Millennium
2000

By Louise L. Hay

Books

The Aids Book: Creating a Positive Approach

Colors & Numbers

Empowering Women

A Garden of Thoughts: My Affirmation Journal

Gratitude: A Way of Life (Louise and Friends)

Heal Your Body

Heal Your Body A–Z

Heart Thoughts: A Treasury of Inner Wisdom

Letters to Louise

Life! Reflections on Your Journey

Love Your Body

Love Yourself, Heal Your Life Workbook

Loving Thoughts for Health and Healing

Loving Thoughts for Increasing Prosperity

Loving Thoughts for a Perfect Day

Loving Thoughts for Loving Yourself

Meditations to Heal Your Life

Millennium 2000 (Louise and Friends)

101 Power Thoughts

101 Ways to Happiness

101 Ways to Health and Healing

The Power Is Within You

You Can Heal Your Life

Coloring Books/ Audiocassettes for Children

Lulu and the Ant: A Message of Love

Lulu and the Dark: Conquering Fears

Lulu and Willy the Duck: Learning Mirror Work

Audiocassettes

AIDS: A Positive Approach

Cancer: Discovering Your Healing Power

Change Your Thoughts, Change Your Life (with Michael Toms)

Elders of Excellence

Empowering Women

Feeling Fine Affirmations

Gift of the Present (with Joshua Leeds)

Heal Your Body (audio book)

Life! Reflections on Your Journey (audio book)

Love Your Body (audio book)

Loving Yourself

Meditations for Personal Healing

Meditations to Heal Your Life (audio book)

Morning and Evening Meditations

Overcoming Fears

The Power Is Within You (audio book)

Self Healing

Songs of Affirmation (with Joshua Leeds)

Tools for Success

What I Believe/ Deep Relaxation

You Can Heal Your Life (audio book)

You Can Heal Your Life Study Course

Conversations on Living Lecture Series

Change and Transition

Dissolving Barriers

The Forgotten Child Within

How to Love Yourself

The Power of Your Spoken Word

Receiving Prosperity

Totality of Possibilities

Your Thoughts Create Your Life

Personal Power Through Imagery Series

Anger Releasing

Forgiveness/Loving the Inner Child

Subliminal Mastery Series

Feeling Fine
Affirmations

Love Your Body
Affirmations

Safe Driving
Affirmations

Self-Esteem Affirmations

Self-Healing
Affirmations

Stress-Free Affirmations

CDs

Self-Healing

Forgiveness/Loving the
Inner Child & Anger
Releasing

Meditations for Personal
Healing/Overcoming
Fears

Self-Esteem Affirmations

Videocassetes

Dissolving Barriers

Doors Opening:
A Positive Approach
to AIDS

Receiving Prosperity

You Can Heal Your Life
Study Course

Your Thoughts Create
Your Life

Also available: *Power
Thought Cards*

All of the above can be ordered
through your local bookstore,
or call or fax:
(760) 431-7695 or (800) 654-5126
(760) 431-6948 (fax) or (800) 650-5115 (fax)
Please visit the Hay House Website at:
www.hayhouse.com

Millennium
2000

A Positive Approach

Louise L. Hay
and Friends

Hay House, Inc.
Carlsbad, CA

Published and distributed in the United States by:
Hay House, Inc., P.O. Box 5100, Carlsbad, CA 92018-5100
(800) 654-5126 • (800) 650-5115 (fax)

Edited by: Jill Kramer   *Designed by:* Jenny Richards

Library of Congress Cataloging-in-Publication Data

Millennium 2000 : a positive approach / Louise L. Hay, [editor] ; and friends.
         p.   cm.
      ISBN 1-56170-658-2 (tradepaper)
       1. Two thousand, A.D.–Psychological aspects.
  2. Millennium–Psychological aspects.
  3. Conduct of life.   I. Hay, Louise L.
  II. Title: Millennium two thousand.
CB161.M478   1999
303.49'09'05–dc21   99-26150
                             CIP

ISBN 1-56170-658-2

02   01   00   99   5   4   3   2
First Printing, May 1999
2nd Printing, June 1999
3rd Printing, August 1999

Printed in Canada

Contents

By Louise L. Hay:

CONTRIBUTORS
(in alphabetical order):

🔊   🔊   🔊

By Louise L. Hay:

🕉   🕉   🕉

Introduction:
The Purpose of This Book

This little book is the result of discussions I've had with friends regarding the nonsense and negativity being disseminated through the media and through various fearmongers about the millennium.

These alarmists could easily be a bigger threat to society than the Y2K issue or any of the other disasters that have been predicted. When we fear the worst, we can easily inflict more serious damage on ourselves, one another, and the economy than anything computers or natural disasters can do. Nobody is going to win if we, as a society, freak out and turn this event into a nightmare.

So many people want to be important and will do anything to have their voices heard. One way to do so is to predict doom and gloom. For example, I was appalled to see a book called *Y2K—It's Already Too Late: Envisioning the Worst in the Year 2000,* by Jason Kelly. Then, my friend Bill Levacy, the Vedic astrologer, told me that many of his clients were expressing concern, wanting to know if the coming millennium would affect them adversely. So, I knew that the fear was definitely out there, and decided that something had to be done to calm people's minds.

I wrote the following letter to several of my friends to see if they would be willing to add their thoughts to this book. The response was very encouraging. I am privileged to have wonderful friends who are willing to support a project such as this one, which will improve the quality of people's lives. So, this little booklet came together. I know that it will help us all to sail into the future with joy.

Dear Friend,

These days, so many people are selling messages of fear and spreading gloom-and-doom predictions about the millennium. It is time for some powerful voices to deliver a message of hope for the coming century shift.

We need to move into the 21st century with a positive concept that things will be better, not worse. This new century will be a reflection of people's hearts and minds. We must be stronger than the fear-mongers, and teach people how to move away from old, fearful thinking. We all have large audiences, and together we can allay the fears that are running rampant all over the planet as the millennium nears.

I am in the process of putting together a small book called _Millennium 2000: A Positive Approach._ It will consist of various messages from powerful voices like yours and mine. It would be wonderful if you could share your vision of the year 2000 with people all over the planet. I will also include many positive affirmations that readers can use to create peace and harmony in their minds as they approach this important date. . . .

Even if you cannot join me in this project, please talk about the posi-

tive new beginnings that the millen-
nium can bring whenever you speak
in public.

Thank you for your time.

Joy and blessings,
Louise

🎴 🎴 🎴

So, my friends and I offer these uplifting concepts to you with love. Read the booklet in its entirety, then each day select some of the affirmations that I've culled from my friends' essays—as well as those I've listed at the end of the book—and keep them in your thoughts. Carry the book in your pocket. Refer to it often, and share it with your friends. In this way, you will rise above any false fears, and you will know and affirm that there is nothing to be afraid of. We are all under the laws of our own consciousness, and we *will* create our own future. So, keep your thoughts clear, and project kind and loving energy. Envision only the best for yourself and for our world in the coming years.

We can now give thanks for the privilege of being on Earth at this pivotal time in history. As we approach the new millennium—letting go of all that doesn't work and repositioning ourselves for a new way of being—we can realize true freedom and empowerment.

Loving Treatments for the New Millennium

I choose a peaceful way of life! Peace begins with me. If I want to live in a peaceful world, then it is up to me to make sure I am a peaceful person. No matter what others may say, do, or even believe, I can keep peace in my heart. I declare peace and harmony in the midst of chaos or even disaster. My thoughts of peace go to every part of the world—past, present, and future. I connect with like-minded peaceful people, and together we march into the millennium knowing that all is well.

🐉　🐉　🐉

I love this planet. I appreciate the beautiful world I live in. This earth is a wise and loving mother and only wants the best for the children who inhabit her body. Everything is provided for my well-being. There is air, water, food, and companionship. I share this planet with an infinite variety of animals, vegetation, birds, fish, and so much incredible beauty. This is where I live; this is my home. I will always help to make it a better place to live. I will contribute to a clean, healthy environment. I go into the 21st century expressing compassion to every person, place, and experience I encounter.

❧ ❧ ❧

My heart is the center of my power. All decisions coming from the loving space of my heart can only benefit the world. The millennium represents a new age and a *new order. I release old, limiting beliefs and old, negative habits. The good that lies before me, that waits for me, can only be reached by a loving, open, caring heart.*

🌀　🌀　🌀

"Remember, dear friends, we have the opportunity to step out of the victim role, and by changing the way we think, become masters of our life. The millennium awaits those who are ready to advance themselves spiritually. If we are willing to release the emotional attachments to beliefs and limitations from the past, then we can live fully in the new moment."

— Louise

🌀　🌀　🌀

❈ ❈ ❈

"Each Christmas for the last three years
I have received the largest, fattest
Amaryllis bulb from Joan Borysenko.
I watch with amazement as it grows into
the most magnificent plant with three or
four large blossoms. I have no idea where
Joan finds these bulbs, perhaps in the
magic kingdom somewhere. I do know
that I am delighted to receive them."

— *Louise L. Hay*

❈ ❈ ❈

I

The Three Jewels of Transformation: Community, Forgiveness, and Compassion

🕉 Joan Zakon Borysenko, Ph.D. 🕉

The dawning of a new millennium is a milestone event, pregnant with the possibility of personal and planetary transformation. All such milestones put us face-to-face with our fears and challenge us to overcome them and arrive at a more expanded, tolerant, forgiving, positive, compassionate, and socially active perspective. Every day we choose whether to heed the paralyzing voice of fear, or to follow the mobilizing inner directives of love. As the millennium approaches, and the attention of over five billion human beings worldwide focuses on our collective hopes and fears for the future, the results of our daily choices become magnified. Many of us feel that our lives are emotionally overwhelmed and chaotic. This flood of feeling is a precious opportunity to overcome negativity and concentrate on developing the three jewels of transformation: *community, forgiveness,* and *compassion.*

We all experience individual milestones—little millennia—that churn up the waters of our lives, bringing both our strengths and hidden fears to the surface. These are vision-birthing times that snap us awake, like a life-challenging illness. They goad us to ask the big questions such as: "What is the purpose of life? What is the legacy of a life well lived? How can I best be of service to others?" The three most potent answers have to do with the importance of community, healing our past through humility and forgiveness, and developing deep compassion for the earth and all living creatures.

Community

In the weeks before I wrote this essay, two friends turned 50. The "decade" birthdays, while a lot less traumatic than illness and millennial fervor, are also "visioning" opportunities—when our inner wisdom calls us to consider life's big questions. One of my friends invited about a dozen of us to sit with her in a "wisdom circle" and share what we felt was most important in the second half of life.

Calling the circle was, in and of itself, a transformative act. It brought the community together in an honest, loving, sometimes humorous, and often moving conversation. It is in sharing our visions, insights, hopes, and fears that we often hear something for the first time ourselves. The intention of meeting in community, whether with a single friend, a small group, or even a large crowd, evokes the space in which our unconscious and superconscious mind can deliver the goodies. It's common to speak and then to wonder, "Where on Earth did that come from?" Together, more powerfully than alone, we can collect the hidden jewels of our life and decide how best to use them. Together we can more honestly and courageously face the task of composting life's garbage so that it can be used as a seedbed for words, thoughts, and deeds in which to grow more conscious, compassionate lives.

Forgiveness

The year 1999 was rare in politics. The president of the United States underwent impeachment hearings as a result of his attempts to cover up his sexual liaison with a young White House intern. A diverse chorus of voices rang out after his acquittal: outrage; disgust at declining moral values or, conversely, that a politician's personal life should have consumed so much time and energy in the first place; relief; and plain old boredom due to the banality of the whole affair. Nonetheless, the sordid drama was a modern-day passion play (no pun intended) that unfolded on the enormous stage of a world linked, for the first time in history, in an instantaneous network of communication.

I'd like to thank President Clinton—not for his actions, but for the symbolic offering of himself as an example of how transformation can proceed only after we've confronted our shadows, owned our dark parts, and begun the process of turning our past mistakes into the compost of a more fertile future in the presence of a community of witnesses. Whether or not one thinks that his apologies were sincere or just empty rhetoric motivated by political angst, it is still inspiring to hear a public figure talk about forgiveness and humility.

In a letter to the cardinals, leaked to the Italian press, the Pope called for a similar exercise in humility and forgiveness, making the point that Christianity had a rare opportunity to own and transform its dark history as we enter a new millennium. If each individual and institution owned its counterpart of the Inquisition, the Crusades, the wiping out of "pagans"—people whose views of reality are different from our own— we would enter the new millennium with hearts attuned more to compassion and community than to isolation and fear. Call me an optimist, but I believe that more and more people and institutions are doing just that. There's a long way to go, but a new world is not built in a single day.

Compassion

When my youngest son, Andrei, was in high school, his social studies teacher assigned an oral history project. Each student interviewed a family elder about their past. Andrei's paternal grandfather shared painful childhood memories of his family's close brush with death in Stalin's holocaust, which killed 12 million Ukrainian people. Ten years later, Andrei's eyes still fill with tears as he recalls his grandfather's story of a neighbor woman who went mad with fear, grief, and starvation. She killed and ate her own young daughter. No amount of reading about Stalin in a history book could conceivably have the same impact in generating a compassionate heart and the strong intent to honor all people and alleviate suffering.

Steven Spielberg founded the Shoah Foundation as an oral history project after hearing many firsthand accounts of survivors of Hitler's holocaust. The foundation is also recording interviews with survivors of the Tibetan, Native

American, and Black holocausts, and is using these moving, first-person accounts to educate students in tolerance and compassion. Holocausts continue the world over. To stop these killings, we must help our children develop not only tolerance for all races, religions and cultures, but the compassionate motivation to support life in all forms, including the ecosystem of our delicate planet.

❊　❊　❊

As we enter the next millennium, we have unprecedented opportunities for both global destruction and global transformation. As I travel the planet learning and teaching, I am convinced that those of us who are asking the big questions about the meaning and purpose of life are a potent, transformative force. We are forming strong transcultural, ecological, and interfaith communities which, only a few decades ago, were unthought of. Our individual and collective skeletons are falling out of the closet. And on those old bones, the living flesh of compassionate respect and conscious social action is growing. Together we can—and I believe we will—realize a world in which the gifts and divinity of every person, and all living things, will be honored and encouraged.

❧   ❧   ❧

*We heal our past with humility
and forgiveness.*

*We collect the hidden jewels of our lives and
decide how best to use them.*

*We turn our past mistakes into the
compost that nourishes the new
seeds we now plant.*

*We own and transform our dark history as
we enter the new millennium.*

*We attune our hearts to compassion
and community.*

*Day by day, we build a new
and better world.*

*We have unprecedented opportunities
for global transformation.*

❈ ❈ ❈

"Carolyn Bratton is a powerful woman whom I have enjoyed knowing for many years. For a long time, wherever I spoke in the world, there was Carolyn in the audience. She teaches my philosophy at her holistic learning center in Roanoke, Virginia, and my column appears in her New Age newspaper, _Lifestream Center._ Whenever she visits me in San Diego, she brings new Feng Shui information to enhance my home. Carolyn even came out for four days to help me while I was moving into my new home. She priced every single item for my garage sale."

— Louise L. Hay

❈ ❈ ❈

II

The Millennium:
A Time for Experiencing
a New Heaven
and a New Earth

🕸 Carolyn A. Bratton 🕸

As we approach this thing called the millennium, I find more and more folks who not only fear what they deem to be perhaps the end of the world as we know it, but who also have fears and unanswered questions about their own destinies. On the other end of the spectrum are folks who don't have a clue what's going on in their own little universe!

I am of the belief that we are approaching a very important time in which we can create a new heaven and a new earth. The millennium, whether real or not (according to Gregorian time, we entered it four years ago!), gives each of us the fabulous opportunity to take a good, long look at how we are living our lives. Are there aspects of our beingness that need adjusting? Have we fulfilled many of our lifelong dreams? Is now the appropriate time to go within and explore the universe that exists within each of us? Can we make time to do the things that bring us real joy and fulfillment? Or are we content to keep going down the same old worn-out path we have been on that has brought us the same old experiences?

I like to think that given this universal burst of energy called the millennium, when everyone on a global basis has the conscious choice to tap into it either positively or negatively, we will know that our belief systems are in for a real test! I see the millennium as a time for great positive change for everyone, because the universal consciousness is moving in that direction. Knowing that each of us is being supported and held in the Light of our choices, we can make a positive difference!

As a Feng Shui consultant/practitioner and the director of a holistic learning center, I have the privilege and constant daily reminder of how people's lives can be changed in a millisecond all because of their willingness to embrace the possibility of change. I think the millennium will help us focus our attention on the positive effects we can consciously bring about for ourselves, our families, and our beautiful Mother Earth—creating that new heaven and new Earth right here, as we live and breathe in our truths.

The only time we have is the eternal present, which seems to turn into the future, but is it, really? We can begin to affect the future—the millennium, if you will, by eternally living in the present. So, let us move forward, working together to create a more loving planet both inside and outside ourselves by affirming the truth of our being: We are all children of a loving God; we are constantly supported by our belief in a Universal consciousness that brings us all we want to experience as our reality; we are loved and

Divinely protected wherever we are; all is well in our lives; and we are truly blessed to be here at this incredible time on our planet.

The Earth is always in constant change—scientists have proven that. We, too, are constantly changing—mentally, physically, emotionally, and cellularly. Change is good; in fact, change is wonderful! As we move into that place of embracing ourselves and our planet more, then we can enjoy all the changes that come. Nothing ever stays the same.

As the millennium approaches, may each of us delight in the possibilities that exist for the expansion of our consciousness for the good of all. And may each of us know that we are all one, and united in the love that is poured out daily on our behalf.

Know that you are loved. God
bless.

*Now is the time to fulfill our
lifelong dreams.*

*We work together to create a more
loving planet.*

*We are loved and Divinely protected
wherever we are.*

*We are so blessed to be here at
this point in time and space.*

The change that lies before us is positive.

*We increase our consciousness
of good in the world.*

❈ ❈ ❈

"You cannot help but love Sylvia Browne when you meet her. She is so down-to-earth and caring. And her predictions are right on. She can remember, word for word, a reading she gave you ten years ago. I know there will come a time in the next millennium when being psychic like Sylvia Browne will be a normal and natural part of life. Everyone will learn how to see into the future, to see in advance the results of our choices, and to guide ourselves accordingly. We will eventually be able to read each other's thoughts, and lying will be a silly habit of the past. We will truly learn to use our thoughts to better our lives. Sylvia Browne has always been a powerful force for good—using her talents and abilities to help those in need."

— **Louise L. Hay**

❈ ❈ ❈

A Loving Look at the Millennium

🕱 Sylvia Browne 🕱

There has been so much hysteria in the print and broadcast media with respect to the year 2000 that it makes many people apprehensive. I have tried my best through my lectures, television appearances, and personal consultations with thousands of clients to quell the fears of the American people.

Psychically as well as spiritually, the world will go on as usual. As it has for millions of years, the sun will rise and set on a world that has long been filled with strife, but it will not be the *end* of the world. Neither the East nor the West Coast will be submerged in water. The computer industry will not collapse. A nuclear war will not occur.

I do feel that this type of negativity brings on many unnecessary heartaches. Fear, after all, is a killer. We know this in the physical body. The earth also has a cell memory just as we do, and negativity begets negativity.

In the year 1000, everyone ran out in the streets ready for the Armageddon. It will surely happen again, and then when nothing catastrophic happens, everyone will go back inside. We have enough to deal with that is negative, so we really must rise above all these doomsday prophecies. After all, our Lord said not once but twice that no man can predict the end.

Let us all band together to educate, help each other, love one another, and heal our sick. This would be a true harmonic convergence. This would truly bring about the age of the Messiah instead of looking to a dark, gloomy future. Besides, if you really study the Gregorian calendar, the year 2000 actually occurred four years ago.

Finally, if the year 2000 is truly going to be the end of the world (which it isn't, but for fantasy's sake, let's pretend it is), what is the very worst thing that could occur? We would just go down that magnificent tunnel to the Other Side together. The only glitch is that the tunnel would be crowded!

Be of good cheer. God loves and protects us, so focus your minds and hearts on positive, loving energy, because this is what God is about.

God love you—*I do.*

   ✦ ✦ ✦

We band together to love one another.

Our love heals all the sickness in the world.

We create a true harmonic convergence.

We rejoice in life and look forward
to a bright future.

We see life with positive, loving eyes.

❦ ❦ ❦

"I met Deepak Chopra in 1995 at a breakfast conference at the American Booksellers' Association convention in Chicago. I was the moderator of the breakfast forum, and it was the first time I had heard him speak. I, like most of the other members at the breakfast, was blown away by his eloquence. I remember saying to the audience at the end of his talk, "You do not have to remember every word Deepak has said. It has all gone into your subconscious mind and will be available to you when you need it." It has always impressed me that Deepak Chopra can speak for four days straight at a workshop without using any notes."

— Louise L. Hay

❦ ❦ ❦

Cloning the Soul?
Will This Happen in
the Next Millennium?

🕉 Deepak Chopra, M.D. 🕉

First a lamb, next a Mahatma? The prospect of cloning a human body has forced buried questions about mind, body, and soul out of the shadows. What if we secured a strand of Einstein's hair—would we be cloning his mind, too? This is enticing and disturbing enough to think about. But why not go further? What if we found a single cell of Jesus' skin—or Buddha's—reposing in a medieval reliquary. Could we clone a soul, and with it a piece of divinity?

I'm suggesting this fantasy or projection—use whatever term you like—because the phrase "cloning the soul" evokes the most disturbing question of all: *Do we even have a soul?* Over the past 11 years, I have given upwards of 1,000 public lectures on diverse topics ranging from mind-body medicine to the afterlife. Whatever the topic, when I throw the floor open to questions, it is the audience's spiritual anxiety that floods over the stage. And that anxiety could have been voiced a hundred, a thousand, or five thousand years ago.

> *Does my life have meaning?*
> *Does God exist?*
> *What happens after I die?*

At the end of this brutal, brilliant century, science is about to deliver us the promise that it has all the answers, at least potentially. Cloning is a symbol of that total victory, that certainty—for even if scientists cannot answer your questions, here is Schweitzer, Einstein, Gandhi, or Darwin to do it for them. Genius on demand is only a step from sainthood on demand. Is this, finally, to be the key to our salvation?

From my experience, science has not advanced our understanding of the soul one inch. This is only reasonable, given that "objective" standards for measuring, weighing, or even detecting the soul have not yet surfaced. Most scientists feel they never will detect it (although the great Indian physicist Chandra Bhose reputedly tried to find the energy charge of the soul—a 20th-century analogy to the medieval physicians who weighed expiring patients to see if they lost a demi-ounce as their soul departed).

The rift between subjectivity and objectivity is too well worn to comment on. But consider this: As far back as 1905, Einstein and the other brilliant quantum pioneers firmly established that reality is wrapped up in the observer. We do not look at the world objectively, as through a plate-glass window; we are woven into it like threads in a tapestry.

Recently I had the privilege of sitting next to Ilya Prigogine, the venerable Belgian Nobel laureate who established important links between patterns and chaos in physical systems. "Do you think," I asked him, "that we might be exploring a universe that is as conscious as ourselves?" Prigogine thought a moment and replied, "Conscious, no— but I believe the universe is creative."

Agreeing with him, I pointed out that the universe that created each of us, through billions of years of evolution, is still inside us, in the form of encoded energy and information. The infinitesimal curlicues of DNA inside each cell could be unwound like a scroll, and written on it would be the history of the cosmos. The infinite fields of energy and intelligence that we all embody are the soul. A soul is pure creativity, pure intelligence, and pure awareness. It transcends time and space by partaking of this moment and all moments, this place and all places. Thus, when the ancient Upanishads declare: "I am That, thou are That, and all this is That," a startling scientific assertion is being made—any quantum physicist working on unified-field theory would agree that a higher-order reality arching over and beyond space-time must exist. Otherwise, the source of the visible universe cannot be explained.

Why, then, does science stand so

firmly as the skeptical gatekeeper who would deny us validation of our soul? Ironically, it's because most scientists have not kept up with their fields. Quantum reality is separated from the soul by no more than the thinnest tissue of a concept. And here is the concept: In a haunting metaphor, the contemporary philosopher and scientist Ken Wilbur has said that humans see with the eyes of the flesh, the eyes of the mind, and the eyes of the soul. Science accepts the first two, but not the third.

We will never know for certain if we can clone the soul until we see through the eyes of the soul. Many already have done this, a loosely confederated pack of poets, visionaries, artists, madmen, and saints. Their experience is just as valid as that obtained through a high-speed particle accelerator. We only have to let it in conceptually. A saint is an objective researcher in his way, as witnessed by St. Augustine: *"And behold You were within me, and I outside myself, and there I searched for You."*

In this age of information, we still haven't shaken off the previous age, dubbed the "Age of Anxiety" by W. H. Auden in a mammoth (126-page) effusion of torment and uncertainty on the eve of World War II. Shall we bring Auden back and ask him if our age has lost its anxiety?

Here I have a prediction to make. An eminent virologist once told me that the AIDS virus remains so mysterious, in part, because of its ability to infiltrate the host cell. "Cells are defended with incredibly elaborate membranes, and inside, the nucleus is guarded like a fortress," he pointed out. "But look at how the entry of a few HIV viruses demolished all that. It's as if someone threw a baseball through the window of the World Trade Center and the whole building collapsed."

The same, I predict, will hold true for "objective" science. It has erected its own huge edifice of knowledge, yet in one window there is a hole. Wind shrieks through that hole; anxiety pours out of it. Everyone notices the hole, but few are willing to talk about it. That hole is the fear of meaninglessness, which only experience of the soul can heal. One day we will be courageous enough to look squarely at that fear, without ridicule, shame, or embarrassment, and then it will be time to build a new edifice, one that will explain the inner universe as confidently as we have now explained the outer. *"And behold You were within me, and I outside myself, and there I searched for You."*

🍥 🍥 🍥

The new Millennium gives our lives great meaning.

The key to our salvation unfolds before us now.

We embody infinite fields of energy and information.

We are pure creativity, pure intelligence, and pure awareness.

❊ ❊ ❊

"Alan Cohen has spent time in my garden basking in the beauty of all the flowers. Of course, mine is a California garden, and he lives in Hawaii, which has a tropical lushness that I cannot match. I discovered that there is a gentle inner warmth to Alan, and he looks at life in a kind and loving way. I would love to have his serenity and peace. But then I wouldn't have Mars in my tenth house."

— **Louise L. Hay**

❊ ❊ ❊

Y Not 2K?

🎇 Alan Cohen 🎇

The question du jour is not, "What do I need to do to protect myself from the coming disaster?" but "What part of the mind—individually and collectively—would take something as bright and beautiful as a new millennium, and try to turn it into a tragedy?"

A Course in Miracles teaches that "pure love calls forth everything unlike itself," and likewise, great change is always perceived as a threat to the fearful mind. But the *Course* also tells us that "all change is good" and that "trust is the bedrock of the entire thought system of the teacher of God."

As I hear more and more talk of chaos on the eve of the new millennium, I see, "en masse," a pattern I have noticed in my own life and that of participants in my workshops. Whenever I am about to make a quantum leap spiritually, socially, or materially, a streak of resistance bubbles forth, screaming, "You can't do that! You're stepping into the unknown! Hold on to the familiar while you still can!"

When I have the presence of mind to move ahead with faith, that shrieking voice is revealed to be not that of Divine guidance, but ancient fear. So I have learned how to make fear my friend; when it shows up, I know I am about to step out of the circle that once circumscribed my world, and discover a bigger universe.

I am not surprised, then, that the

changing of a year, decade, century, and millennium should call forth massive unrest. I am reminded of a time when I was about to move from one house to another and I had cleared all of my furniture out of my living room. My dog, sensing that the world she had known was now in disarray, became extremely nervous, and, in an uncustomary manner, chased my car down the driveway when I made a simple trip to the store. She did not realize that all was well, that change was good, and that the next home she would live in would offer her an even bigger yard and more room to play.

What does surprise me is the extent to which spiritually mature people are selling out to hype and hysteria. Recently I attended a party where Y2K took over the discussion. The energy field suddenly became infiltrated with the vibration of sensationalism, self-defensiveness, and small-mindedness. In contrast to the loving and empowering discussion that preceded it, lack, powerlessness, and personal interests dominated; and speakers took macabre pleasure in gloating over alleged statistics of the backlog in generator availability, how much money Bank of America is paying to ward off Y2K woes, and minutiae of previous obscure computer failures. Calmly, I left the room.

I have come too far on my spiritual path to meander down the highway of fear. Many years ago, I studied with a teacher who made many authoritative predictions about the end times to come. Claiming to have been psychically visited by Nostradamus, the teacher issued dates and gory details of many worldwide calamities and disasters that would take place between 1981 and 2000. Motivated largely by fear and self-protection, more than a hundred students got together and formed a survival community. We purchased land in a remote area, dug and built underground bunkers, buried huge gas tanks, and bought tons of survival food. I was personally responsible for ordering the food, which eventually filled a barn. We worked long and hard to ready ourselves for economic collapse, worldwide famine, and nuclear fallout. Thank God we never got guns.

One day after about five years, I had two sudden realizations: (1) I had sold my faith out to fear, and as I immersed myself in protection from a future disaster, I was missing out on the beauty and abundance available in that moment; and (2) the predictions that the teacher had made for that time period had not come to pass. I decided there had to be more to life than living in a cold, dank bunker; and that I would rather live in joy, appreciation, and celebration than protect myself from a looming dooms-day. Peacefully, I left.

Twenty years have come and gone since the day the end of the world was announced. None of the teacher's pre-dictions have materialized. The teacher was sincere, and truly sought to help the students build a better world. But the information was incorrect. Either it came from a faulty source, or there was a consciousness shift that changed the dynamics of the game.

But there was a hidden blessing. I loved being part of a spiritual commu-nity. I loved working side by side with my peers, and, aside from the disaster scenario, we had great times—we sang, meditated, laughed, and grew together as a family. I look back on those community years as some of the most nourishing of my life. Now I think hardly at all about the survival element, but I reminisce very fondly about the family element. So in the long run I gained a great deal—not from the disaster, but from the love.

We don't need to scare ourselves to get together. Been there, done that, bought the T-shirt, and it's too small. But we can look fear in the eye and ask, "What is the deeper lesson here?"

My friend Jerry spends his days in a wheelchair and receives modest financial support from the government. He told me that he was feeling anxious about Y2K, for if government computers go down, he will lose his source of support. I suggested to Jerry that he has a source of support far more powerful than the government. Since his injury five years ago, volunteers from our community have provided Jerry with help every day, and organized massive fundraisers. Jerry is supported by the Almighty God, currently channeled partly through the government, and much more through friends and other miraculous avenues. If God has taken such good care of him thus far, I told Jerry, I have every reason to expect that goodness and mercy shall continue to follow him.

And so will it be for all of us. All is well, and there is nothing to fear. As Divine beings, we are imbued by our Creator with wisdom, guidance, and creativity via our internal spiritual computers; time and again we have demonstrated awesome ingenuity. We engineered our way to the moon using a computer no more sophisticated than an old Commodore 64 (a toy!). And we later wrested Apollo 13 from the jaws of disaster using socks and chewing gum. Since we invented the computer, I figure we can easily solve a problem as minute as a couple of computer digits. The solution may take a few bucks, but we can afford it; we live in a prosperous universe, and if God gives us a task, God will give us the means to accomplish it. Y2K is easily solvable if we keep our heads in the right place and refrain from using this challenge as a distraction from the Kingdom at hand.

We can use the fearful Y2K scenarios presented to us to practice either the presence of God, or His/Her absence; we will make of it whatever we choose. Why would anyone argue in favor of disaster when he or she could make a stand for well-being? For 2,000 years, we have kept Jesus on the cross emulating and reenacting his crucifixion in our lives—a practice entirely in contradiction of his teachings. I think the 2000-year point would be a perfect opportunity to finally take Jesus down from the cross, and ourselves along with him. We do not have to create a drama of suffering to earn salvation; we need simply to acknowledge the perfection within and around us.

So I say, "Bring on the millennium!" My vision is that we will open our eyes on the morning of January 1, 2000, and live not in a darkened world, but a brightened one. The light by which we live is produced not by electric companies, but by the radiance of our hearts, minds, and spirits. Jesus advised us, "You are the light of the world; do not hide your light under a basket." Or a computer.

❁ ❁ ❁

All is well; there is nothing to fear.

We live in a prosperous universe.
We make a stand for well-being
in the world.

We acknowledge the perfection within
and around us.

Bring on the millennium!

⟡ ⟡ ⟡

"Terah Kathryn Collins and I are laughing friends. We are always excited to see each other. We love to get in my pick-up truck and go on adventures. We once went to a worm factory and came home with a truckload of worm castings (worm poop) for our gardens. Terah even brought me a bowl of fresh worms when I moved to my new home. We often go plant hunting. We once went to a llama ranch, spending the day with these glorious animals. She is such a great teacher. I love taking classes at her Feng Shui school."

— Louise L. Hay

⟡ ⟡ ⟡

Outer Simplicity,
Inner Richness

❖ Terah Kathryn Collins ❖

The millennium is a new beginning for all of us; it's the closing of one door and the opening of another. In the last thousand years of evolution, humanity has gone from being many disconnected tribes, to being one vast, interconnected family. Now as we stand at the threshold of the 21st century, we have the opportunity to improve the quality of life for every member of this global family.

Look back 1,000 years and see how much we've evolved. We can look toward the future's horizon and glimpse the dawning of planetary peace. We can hope our descendants will look back from the year 3000 and say, "We have created a heavenly Earth. Through our efforts over the last 1,000 years, we now live long, healthy, and happy lives, honoring and celebrating the diversity of life." With this vision of the future guiding us, our present task is to explore and practice ways of living that contribute *now* to greater harmony in our world.

Feng Shui—the study of the connection between seen and unseen forces of nature—gives us important guidelines on how to participate and contribute in a positive way to this vision. The first guideline is to practice simplicity. Live with the possessions that you genuinely need and that give you joy, and let go of the rest. In so doing, you "share the wealth" and help to balance supply and demand. By focusing on quality, not quantity, your possessions become Environmental Affirmations that support and enhance your health, happiness, and prosperity.

The second Feng Shui guideline is to practice being in relationship. Claim your connection with everyone and everything on the planet by creating positive, nurturing relationships with yourself, your neighbors, and your community. By loving yourself and others, you contribute to the overall health and well-being of our global family.

The third Feng Shui guideline is to embrace change. Change moves us forward to greater expressions in life, including building peaceful, environmentally friendly communities where all species are honored and given a home. Ask yourself, "How can I change for the better? How can I simplify my life and serve my community? Do I need to settle any disputes; or become more loving, forgiving, and grateful for the life I live on this beautiful planet?"

The new millennium invites us to look within and to develop the personality and character traits that give harmony a place to live. This inner focus is already happening. Many of us are already more attracted to inner qualities than outer appearances. Ultimately, we will all practice simplicity, cultivate loving relationships, and celebrate change while pursuing the development of inner qualities such as creativity, compassion, forgiveness, generosity, and gratitude.

As we enter the new millennium, let each of us embrace our part in creating a generous, peaceful, and prosperous global family!

We now improve the quality of life for every
member of our global family.

We live with only those things that
make our hearts sing.

We welcome change and celebrate
the diversity of life.

We simplify our lives and serve
our communities.

We choose to live in a generous, prosperous, happy, healthy, loving world.

We glimpse the dawning of planetary peace,
and begin to create a heavenly Earth.

"Dr. Tom and I are traveling buddies. We met in the Los Angeles airport on our way to Hong Kong many years ago. We spent almost the whole tour together and became fast friends. This year we flew to Moscow and spent two weeks on a river cruise up the Volga to St. Petersburg. Wherever we go, Tom is always greeted with love. On the rare occasions when I get to visit his church, I am always delighted to see how loved he is. The members of his congregation adore him, and so do I."

— Louise L. Hay

VII

J.E.A.R.
(False Evidence Affecting Reality)

❧ Dr. Tom Costa ❧

I like to use acronyms in my writings. To me, the word *fear* as an acronym stands for False Evidence Affecting Reality. I don't doubt that there will have to be some adjustments required on the part of the many companies making the computer systems. However, the same Mind that created the computer is the same Mind that can solve the problems and readjust, reorganize, and recompute information. The Reality (a capital *R* for God) can certainly deal with the reality (lower-case *r*) that we humans create.

One of my favorite spiritual affirmations, which works not only in the computer world, but also in every problem with which I am confronted, has helped me in times of my need for recomputation in every area of my life. The only time I truly have trouble is when I forget this statement of Truth.

The affirmation is:

I'M VERY INTERESTED TO SEE HOW MIND WORKS THIS OUT!

The word *THIS* in the above statement stands for any problem in the Universe that we might be facing. When we let Mind work it out in a way we know not how, glorious answers begin to appear out of that proverbial blue.

In understanding the above affirmation, we are able to become more objective, and we are able to stand back and allow this One Mind, this Great Unseen that we call God, to work IT out. As Emerson said, "We must get our bloated nothingness out of the way." This is another way of saying "let go and let God" fill in the details. How much wasted precious time shall be wasted on the glitches that *might* be caused in the new millennium. If it is really a new period of time, then the answer to the glitches will also be new. The answer is already known in the Mind of God. The answer is always simple when it is known.

Realistically, I do not doubt that something needs to be done, but at the same time, I believe that it *shall* be done at exactly the right time in exactly the right way—perfectly, Divinely, and magnificently.

I pose the question: *Is there anything that the one Mind, God, cannot do?* I personally cannot think of anything. The only time that my life is glitched is when I forget that Truth.

❧ ❧ ❧

*The Mind that created us is the same
Mind that will take us into the new century.*

*The intelligence of the universe
sees us through.*

Glorious answers appear out of the blue.

*New solutions are available for
new questions.*

We rejoice in a happy new millennium.

❦ ❦ ❦

"I have always been so impressed
with Shakti Gawain. Her book
Creative Visualization was a landmark
work and set the stage for so much good in
the world. Also, I really admire the way
that Shakti knows how to enjoy both her
work and her play, which I do, too. She
and her husband, Jim, make their home in
Hawaii, and manage to run both a
successful business and indulge
in the wonderful pleasures that
the islands have to offer."

— **Louise L. Hay**

❦ ❦ ❦

VIII

The Path of Transformation: How Healing Ourselves Can Change the World

🕉 Shakti Gawain 🕉

As we rapidly approach the new millennium, life on our planet seems to be intensifying. Most of us are faced with challenging personal problems—in our jobs, our relationships and families, our finances, and our health. We're not sure how to best meet these challenges. Our traditional ways of living, working, and relating to each other and our environment don't seem to be functioning very well anymore, yet we have few role models for effective new ways.

Even more overwhelming are the problems confronting humanity as a whole. On a planetary level, things seem to be getting worse and worse. We wonder why there is so much pain, suffering, and struggle all over the world. Most of us have no idea what we can do to help, so we do little or nothing.

Today's challenges can only be met powerfully and effectively through a shift in consciousness, which in fact is already well under way worldwide. We need to recognize, to the depths of our souls, that we are all part of one whole, that what each of us does individually has a powerful impact on us all. By making a commitment to your own consciousness journey, you are indeed taking a significant role in the transformation of the world.

Most people reading this book will agree that the time has come for profound transformation in our lives and in the world. Indeed, this transformation is already under way. But the questions arise, "How can we support and contribute to that process? How can we do our part, as individuals, to make sure it's going in a positive direction? How do we create real change in our personal lives and in the world?"

The simple answer to that question is this: *We change the world most effectively by changing our own consciousness*. There is a quote attributed to Mohandas Gandhi that says this well: "You must be the change you wish to see in the world." As each of us becomes more aware on an individual level, we see change reflected in our personal lives. Old problems and patterns gradually melt away, and we meet new difficulties and challenges with a widening perspective and increasing wisdom. Our lives become more balanced, more fulfilling, and more in alignment with our soul's purpose. Since each one of us is an integral part of the collective consciousness, we each have a subtle but powerful effect on that mass consciousness (and vice versa). Like the proverbial pebble dropped into a still pond, the shifts of consciousness we make in our personal lives send out tiny but important waves that ripple over the surface of the whole.

When we, as individuals, grow in consciousness, the mass consciousness

shifts accordingly. As the mass consciousness changes, it pulls along other
individuals who may be clinging to old
patterns, or who are simply unaware of
how to proceed. So as a few wake up,
everyone begins to awaken. And as the
collective consciousness expands, the
social, economic, and political forms of
the world respond to those new levels
of awareness.

Changing our lives and changing
the world cannot be accomplished
either by focusing exclusively on exter-
nal solutions or by following a traditional transcendent, spiritual path in
which the reality and importance of the
physical world is minimized or denied.
Rather, we need to choose an alterna-
tive that I call the path of transformation, in which we commit ourselves to
the integration of our spiritual and

human aspects and learn to live as whole beings, in balance and fulfillment on the earth.

Human life consists of four levels of being—spiritual, mental, emotional, and physical. The path of transformation involves clearing, healing, developing, and integrating all four of these levels. They are all equally important, and there isn't one that we can skip or neglect if we want to experience wholeness. As we do so, all four levels naturally begin to balance, and they become more fully integrated with one another.

We may begin our consciousness journey at any one of these levels, as each person's path is unique. Once we have begun, we may move from one level to another at different times; or we may work on two, three, or all four levels simultaneously. Generally, however, no matter where we start our consciousness journey, or how we proceed with it, there's a certain underlying evolutionary process that unfolds from the spiritual to the physical. (For more about this journey toward wholeness, please see my books *The Path of Transformation: How Healing Ourselves Can Change the World*; and *The Four Levels of Healing: Balancing the Spiritual, Mental, Emotional, and Physical Aspects of Your Life*.)

Envisioning the Future Together

I'd like to invite you to join me and all the other readers of this book in envisioning the future. I'm going to ask you to close your eyes and imagine it.

Pay special attention to your most creative fantasies. If doubts and fears come up, acknowledge them and allow them to be there, too. Then turn your attention to developing your vision. Don't limit it in any way. Allow it to be as expansive as you would like.

Get in a comfortable position with your pen and paper, journal, crayons, or whatever tools you'd like within easy reach. Close your eyes and take a few, slow, deep breaths. Let your awareness move into a quiet place deep inside of you. Ask yourself, "What is my vision of the future?"

First, focus your attention on imagining your own personal future as you would most like it to be. If you're not quite sure how you want it to be, just allow yourself to go with one fantasy about it, knowing that you can change it whenever you want to. Imagine your relationship with yourself as fulfilling as possible on all four levels. Imagine everything in your life reflecting the balance and harmony within your own being—your relationships, your work, your finances, your living situation, and your creative pursuits. Allow them all to be wonderfully successful and satisfying.

Now expand your focus to imagine the future of the world around you— your community, your country, humanity, the natural environment, and our planet. Allow them all to reflect the integration and wholeness you have found within yourself. Imagine the new world emerging and developing in a healthy, balanced, expansive way. Really let your imagination soar. Envision the world as you would love it to be—a paradise on Earth.

When you feel complete with the process, open your eyes. If you wish, write or draw your vision. Thank you for joining me. Bless you.

❦ ❦ ❦

A positive shift in consciousness
is taking place worldwide.

As we heal ourselves, we heal the planet.

Our lives become more balanced, more
fulfilling, and more in alignment
with our soul's purpose.

We choose the path of transformation,
and we learn to live as whole beings.

In this new millennium, our journey
is toward wholeness.

The new world is emerging in a healthy,
balanced, expansive way.

❧ ❧ ❧

"I fell in love with this beautiful Haitian lady the instant I met her at a seminar given by Dr. Christiane Northrup. I saw a powerful, alive, vivacious, and eloquent woman who also happened to be a medical doctor. The more I learned about this fascinating woman and her life story, the better friends we became. Carolle loves life with a passion, and she brings joy to every room she enters. Her patients are very privileged to have her as their physician. She is the author of <u>Menopause Made Easy</u> and <u>Staying Healthy: 10 Easy Steps for Women</u>."

— Louise L. Hay

❧ ❧ ❧

The New Millennium:
A Better Time for
Humanity

🔯 Carolle Jean-Murat, M.D. 🔯

Many predictions are being made about the advent of the coming millennium. Some people forecast dire warnings of social collapse, others predict cataclysms, yet others predict a new golden age. I haven't a prediction so much as an expectation: The world is going to be a better place because people are becoming more informed. They are learning more about the interrelatedness of all things and discovering how each of life's facets impinges on or impacts them personally.

One area that has remained in the shadows for generations is women's health—specifically, the midlife changes that occur around menopause. I've observed that female baby boomers are coming into their own, recognizing and capitalizing on their individual and unique power. They are opting for more satisfying relationships in all areas of their lives. Specifically, their focus has shifted toward developing a quality of life that engenders a deeper sense of personal success and contentment. Since the onset of the women's movement of the '60s, there have been two noticeable trends of note: (1) Women have become more proactive in the management of their health as they mature; and (2) older women are vesting the next generation by providing greater support and guidance for younger women. Perhaps an offshoot of these trends is the rise in the number of people volunteering for charities. Between 1987 and 1995, the number has doubled.

What women are acting upon is the simple need to become better informed—about what really matters to them, and about the life changes promulgated by menopause. Women are seeking to understand and have control over the physical/hormonal changes starting around age 40 that necessitate modifications in lifestyle, sexuality, diet, exercise, and therapeutic approaches. Life becomes far more complicated due to age; this important midlife change; and the increased potential for osteoporosis, heart disease, and various types of cancer. Compounding this period in a woman's life is a great deal of confusing and conflicting information—and a lack of substantial research.

For years, research funding has been reserved for men, with the resultant findings extrapolated to women. The prevailing thinking was that women's hormonal changes were considered to "skew" research results. Fortunately, the new millennium will see the first major breakthrough in women's and, specifically, minorities' health research. This is due to the research being done by the Women's Health Initiative; the findings are scheduled for release in the year 2005. Consequently, the influence of racial, cultural, and economic factors in the health of postmenopausal women will be more clearly defined.

The next step for the Initiative will be the dissemination of its findings. One such medium women will be able to utilize is the Internet, where information and support are readily available either at home, in the workplace, or through the public library. It offers chat rooms, clubs, and websites that allow women to fully explore the parameters and stages of this roller-coaster period.

Other important factors that require consideration are the compounding environmental stresses that women all over the world may face on a daily basis. For myself, growing up in Haiti, there were a number of major obstacles that I now realize were challenges that I had to come to terms with—and they helped me become the person I am today. To begin with, women in my mother country were considered second-class citizens; therefore, the opportunities afforded were meager and required the utmost in determination, inner strength, and focus. Haiti is now the poorest nation in the Western Hemisphere. Poverty is endemic. In short, my country needs help from those who understand its people, its culture, and the potentials for its future—people who want to "make a difference."

As a doctor practicing for more than 20 years in the United States, I have provided medical care and preventive health education to women of diverse backgrounds. Additionally, I have for over a decade provided free medical care to under-served women through Catholic charities, The Salvation Army, and St. Vincent de Paul Village in San Diego. I have sought throughout my career to do what I can to alleviate, uplift, support, educate, and empower women in the United States. My dream for the millennium is to do the same for my brothers and sisters in Haiti. A project I've chosen is the creation of a center called "The Center for Learning and

Giving." My dream for this center is to have a primary school, a vocational school for young adults, an outpatient clinic, a nursing school, a convalescent home, a minor surgery center, and eventually a hospital. At the center, all children and young adults who come through its doors will be provided the resources to help them reach their full potential, and will then be encouraged to return to help others. I envision people from all over the world coming together to make this dream a reality—not for me, but for the people of Haiti, its underprivileged, and the children of its 21st-century future.

There were a number of people who impacted my life. I know that I have the power, skills, strength, and life experience to turn around and do the same for others. They deserve everything I have to offer.

As I stated earlier, many people are hoping for a new golden age. All I can say is that life is grand—right now! I have a wonderful career, profound relationships, loving friends, and am having the time of my life. Meeting Louise L. Hay has been a major blessing for me. She has "made a difference" for hundreds of thousands of people through her life example and her love. She is a woman of enormous depth and dimension. More women of her caliber are needed to step forward and make a difference in this world. Together, we can all step into the coming millennium, knowing that the world will be a better place for all humanity—one step at a time, heart by heart, empowering each day with the strength of our convictions. We have nowhere to go but up!

Here we come, year 2000!

*We create a world of personal success
and contentment.*

*The new millennium brings a major
breakthrough in women's health.*

*We envision people from all over the
world coming together in peace.*

*The world deserves everything we
have to offer.*

Life is grand right now!

*The world is becoming a better place
for all humanity.*

"When the time is right and the student is ready, the teacher appears. Meeting Bill Levacy was a destiny thing. I have learned so much from him. In fact, he was the main motivation behind this book. I shared my concern with him about the millennium fearmongers, and he told me that many of his clients were apprehensive about the dawning of the 21st century. In my opinion, he is one of the best astrologers I've ever met. Before Bill, I was not even aware of Vedic Astrology. Now I am constantly amazed by how accurate his predictions are for me. Sometimes he will say something as a joke, and it turns out to be right on."

— **Louise L. Hay**

The Millennium Trap

🕸 William R. Levacy 🕸

As we turn the corner into the next century, we see the media saturated with the points of view of a small but vocal group of individuals. These "Millennialists," as recently dubbed by ABC News, have learned the skills to manipulate and direct the awareness of gullible people to noisy and extreme situations. These individuals and groups have developed expertise in manufacturing gloom and communicating exaggeration. An inordinate amount of time has been given to their alarming messages, rather than to those that alert, empower, and uplift the population about the millennium ahead. God bless these folks, but they are not kind to our times and have led many of us to have a scary and unhealthy relationship with the future. I hold that it is still popular and useful to be hopeful, and most negative forecasters, if they are willing to be honest, will be embarrassed, if not amused, in the 21st century by what they said in the 20th.

Before we go too far, I would like to say that I have been involved in the "art" of forecasting since 1982 when I began the study of Vedic Astrology, the science of behavior and time developed in ancient India. Some say that *Jyotish,* as this style of astrology is also called, was first recorded some 6,000 years or so ago and has most likely existed in an oral format for several thousand years more. One of Vedic Astrology's first sages, Maharishi Parashara, revealed many techniques for recognizing and aligning oneself to the life-supporting forces of nature.

As an astrologer, looking ahead, I see time for the creation of a new order of things. The sidereal conjunction of Saturn and Jupiter in Aries on May 28, 2000, can rise up to push out much of the negative activities in countries around the world. We should see a higher level of rightness and order. This astrological event promises to mark a time of restoration rather than destruction. A new legislative balance should prevail, and an overall beneficial transformation of societal structure should take place.

Jupiter and Saturn are not hot-heads—they are purveyors of lawfulness. During the next few years, the more warlike planets at that time, such as Mars and the north node of the Moon (called *Rahu* in Sanskrit), are not in any dominant position to steer the times toward any major trouble. The nations of the world might still have their sibling and neighborly rivalries and disputes as they work to manage local differences—as in any age—but not to a devastating, global degree.

The last time Saturn and Jupiter were strongly associated, in this case by opposition, we witnessed the fall of the Berlin Wall, the end of Soviet Communism, and the Cold War—a situation no one thought possible at the time. Another point taken as a sign of doom by alarmists is the multi-planet conjunction occurring in the sidereal Aries around the morning of the 5th of May in 2000. We've had multi-planet conjunctions like this before, such as February 6, 1962, and believe it or not, we're still here. This early May 2000 conjunction can generate a crackling spark to increase the energies of the world. I propose that this force be captured as a flare for the dark, sluggish, or disregarded sectors of the world economy to move forward with renewed light and vigor. Technological and medical advances could be made at this time—the lively machines of invention, renewal, and humanitarian efforts—rather than those of war.

The establishment of this new order in the 21st century, while not guaranteed to be silky smooth, need not be married to any disaster scenarios, as some astrologers and other prognosticators are suggesting. There is not enough negative mass from the recent past to generate the degree of troubled times we saw in the early to middle decades of the 20th century. In fact, I believe we have already seen a lot of pent-up tensions diffused in the world, with recent events such as the Gulf War; the troubles in Yugoslavia; the

Northridge, California, earthquake; Hurricane Mitch; the Malibu, California, fires; the cold freeze in the Northeast U.S., and so on. There is not enough negative collateral left for successful deployment of a perpetually dismal or cataclysmic future. We should be listening for the heralds of peace, and not for the nuisance and nonsense of panicked or exhausted persons.

It is also important to note that Vedic philosophy speaks of *Yugas*, or major time epochs, the end of each culminating in dissolution and setting the stage for a new era. According to the Yuga theory, we have more than 427,000 years to go before any possible type of major correction. We can put annihilation out of the picture for the new century, no matter how popular it may be for certain groups (they're dying to die). However, the New Age and current Yuga require a style of vigilance, resourcefulness, and genuineness well within the will and capacity of the major stakeholders of the 21st century. Additionally, in another 400 years or so, we will have the Spring Equinox occurring in the sidereal sign of Aquarius—an inventive, technological, and philosophically robust period of time. The boat to the new millennium does not need to heave forward onto heavy seas, dodging icy monsters. It can float briskly into the warm, new waters ahead—captained by excited, dexterous, and watchful seamen and seawomen who, cooperatively, have their eyes on the stars.

I would like to emphasize that the future is as good as we want it to be. I think an old joke is appropriate here: "The future is not what it used to be." We can see that the fundamentals that guided the last generation are not as effective in today's environment. We

have most of the baby boomers antici-
pating a promising future for themselves (and getting it) and paying less
attention to the negative side. Many of
the older thinking patterns are being
transformed. We are effortlessly dis-
missing these concepts as being less
evolved—much to the consternation of
their proponents. The fresher, unlimit-
ed, yet tender thought of today's
younger minds is dominant and starting
to press its shape on the future.

As we enter the new millennium, we
need to be alert to the wisdom of our
predecessors, and we have to be careful
to realize that the *future* is not the *past*.
That is why they are different words.
The past is the past, and the future is
the future. We must not let unhappy or
despairing persons—no matter what
their level in society—alarm us with
their negative projections. We must also
realize that the doomsday prophecies

we might be hearing come tinged with a lot of hidden agendas, and are from people who might be tired of coping and are afraid themselves.

The marketplace in the wisdom business is very crowded these days— filled with consultants, ministers, psychics, astrologers, and other futurists. Noise makes news, so the more aggressive, if not irresponsible, players in the knowledge field look at some way to distinguish themselves from the crowded pulpits of their peers.

Even astrologers and forecasters of some repute, tasting some increased renown in displaying their predictive abilities, would be best advised to show respect for the future and forego giving weight to some anticipated disasters in the name of the well-being of the public. At the very least, people help the most when they talk of problems in terms of solutions. The best astrologers guide people to their highest destinies—they inform them but don't scare them. I believe, for example, that the Y2K computer "problem" is real to a degree, but not to the disastrous levels projected by those selling software and survival gear solutions—not to mention the scanty and tweaked research offered as the narrow footing for some extremist philosophical and religious theories. We have all heard of false hope. I would like to counter that, in all fairness, there can also be false despair.

From my practice as an astrologer, I find that these non-affirming people are stuck on pessimistic projections and can't get these thoughts out of their heads. They are too attached to their pre-planned goals. These individuals usually need to develop the ability to accept natural obstacles and find more appropriate solutions. I find that about 90 percent of what nervous people worry about doesn't happen, and that they are quite capable of handling the other 10 percent. They should stop scaring themselves and those who are easily frightened.

We need to identify ourselves as bright, intelligent, resourceful, and hopeful subscribers to the new millennium. I believe that God is not a practical joker and has given us all the will and the capacity to choose a good future for ourselves. We need to call the bluff on the negativists. They have exceeded the threshold in projecting a troubled future, and have overstayed their time in the broadcast booth.

I encourage us all to respond with a positive and hearty voice as we call out to the next millennium and set the scene for the many good years that lie ahead. Increase and sustain your competency through education (the future requires more learning), redesign your hearts, and learn to meditate to stay calm. Linger in the company of cheerful people. Use tools such as astrology to help you avert any problems that lie ahead. Eat your vegetables. Be good to your friends. Learn to love and to take action. Be happy in your work, and stay close to the natural way of things. Prance. Above all, transmit positive signals to the future, and strengthen the connection between what is good now, and all the good that is to come.

The future needs you!

*There is a positive new energy
for the 21st century.*

We listen for heralds of peace.

Optimism is becoming popular.

*The boat to the new millennium
floats on peaceful seas.*

*Older thinking patterns are
being transformed.*

We are quite capable of handling each day.

*We choose a promising future
for ourselves.*

＊ ＊ ＊

"I first met Dr. Christiane Northrup through her book <u>Women's Bodies, Women's Wisdom.</u> I read it in two days, all 700 or so pages. The excitement I felt while reading this book was hard to contain. Never before had anyone addressed the subject of women's health in such a supportive way. I began to recommend her book to everyone I knew, close friends and those at my lectures. When I met Chris in person, I was delighted to experience her wonderful sense of humor. The two years we spent together doing the Empowering Women seminars were a joy and a delight. I always learn something from her whenever we meet. She has definitely become a mentor of mine."

— **Louise L. Hay**

＊ ＊ ＊

XI

Saying Good-bye to the 1900s: Preparing to Enjoy the New Millennium

🕸 Christiane Northrup, M.D. 🕸

With the computer glitch known as Y2K looming ahead as the 20th century draws to a close, all of us will be faced with what I consider the most significant choice of our lives: to remain locked into the dysfunctional patterns of fear and limitation we learned in childhood—fears symbolized by Y2K anxiety—or to move ahead into the boundless energy of freedom, growth, and joy that is becoming more available than ever before.

I'm excited by the coming new millennium, and I feel intuitively that it will usher in a new era in which a very significant proportion of the population will learn how to apply the laws of the universe to their daily lives, making life more fun, creative, abundant, and joyful than ever before. Two examples of the laws of the universe are the Law of Attraction, which states that like attracts like; and the Law of Abundance, which states that there is more than enough to go around.

The Law of Attraction teaches us that what we attract into our lives matches the energy we put forth. Our surroundings and the people in our lives are a direct reflection of our beliefs. If you look around and like what you see, chances are you've learned how to tap into this law consciously. If you don't like what you see, however, you still have the power to change your life by changing your beliefs a little at a time. The Law of Abundance states that the universe is a place of limitless abundance. To participate consciously in the truth of this law, you need to feel completely worthy of receiving on all levels. Depending upon your circumstances, it may take you some time to allow a deep sense of your own worthiness into your life.

If you are not consciously working with universal laws at this time, the coming millennium will give you more opportunities than ever to do so. Why? Because as a light gets lighter, the dark gets darker. That means it will become increasingly difficult to hold on to burdensome patterns of any kind that don't allow you to become all of who you are if (and this is a big "if") any part of you claims to believe in the role of consciousness, the mind/body connection, or any other example of the link between consciousness and matter. (If you don't believe in that connection, you're probably not reading this. If your mother doesn't believe in it, but you do, don't bother to give her this essay. It probably won't do anything but aggravate her.)

The medical intuitive Caroline Myss teaches that the degree to which we're vulnerable to illness depends to a great extent on the difference between what we say we believe and how we actually live our lives. So, for instance, if you say you believe in the mind/body connection but then excuse yourself from taking responsibility for your next illness by saying that it "just happened" or you "caught something," then you are not walking your talk, and you'll be giving double messages to the cells in your body and to the universe. Conflicting beliefs put out mixed messages, thereby producing mixed results. Never fear, though, the energy of completion and new beginnings that is being ushered in with the new millennium will bring these patterns to the surface for healing.

While the ambivalence within us is being flushed out in many of us, however, there are and will continue to be relatively healthy individuals whose lives and beliefs are internally consistent in that they don't even pretend to believe in universal law, the effects of consciousness, or the mind/body connection. If, for example, you are 80 years old, generally happy with your life, are surrounded by like-minded individuals, and haven't felt the need to update your beliefs or your life much since 1950, then you aren't likely to suffer much. We all know individuals like this who started smoking at the age of 13, have a few drinks every night, love their lives, and honestly believe that cigarettes and their daily slug of brandy are important and essential parts of their health-care regimen! And for them, it works quite well.

On the whole, the coming new century will increasingly see the world divided into three groups: Group A, the consciousness-based folks, will notice that their lives keep getting better and better (maybe worse for a while, but then much better). Group B are those still planted firmly in the world in which the only universal law that is recognized is the law of gravity. They also believe that Divinity is a force outside themselves. This is the group consisting of the survivalists who honestly believe that the best solution to the challenge of the next millennium is to wall themselves up in an armed camp somewhere in a remote area. Group C is perhaps the largest group. It is an in-between one that is currently undecided, but more or less open to the idea that there must be something more than gravity and a vengeful God running the planet. The individuals in this group will waffle back and forth between believing that consciousness creates reality, versus feeling like victims of the universe. Some will eventually join Group A, and some will migrate to Group B if their fear overcomes their faith.

These three groups and the consciousness they represent were not nearly as distinct back in 1950, although they were present. But now time is moving more quickly than it did back then. It's nearly impossible to stay in one place for long. Notice that our grandparents tended to marry once and live in the same place for a lifetime. They also usually had only one occupation during their lives. Now, people have two or three careers, move on the average of once every five years, and they may marry a couple or more times over the course of their lives. Today, as compared to 20 years ago, it takes much less time for our thoughts to manifest into physical reality than it did back in the 1950s. The spiritual teacher known as Abraham says that it only takes 17 seconds of uninterrupted pure positive thought on a subject to effect a physical manifestation, whereas 20 or so years ago it took longer. The effects of our thoughts on matter and the events of our lives are easier to see than ever before, and this will continue.

The year 1999 began with the rare

event of two full moons in January, the last one being a "blue moon." This won't happen again for more than 30 years. Full moons represent the unconscious and illuminate the shadow sides of our lives and personalities. So right from the beginning, 1999 began with two full moons, twice the usual celestial opportunity to identify and clean up any patterns of behavior that are no longer serving our highest and best purpose. An entire century, which included two world wars, is now drawing to a close, and the baby boomers—that huge chunk of the population who were nurtured with more security and wealth than any previous generation—are now moving into midlife and imbuing positions of power and authority with a more open and spiritually aware consciousness. Nothing will ever be the same. So get ready.

How to Lighten Your Load for the
New Millennium

Here's the best way I know to get
the universe to help you take out the
trash of your personal and professional
life so that you'll be really ready to let
in, and dance with, the increasing
amount of light that is coming our way:

**1. Utilize the amazing power of
focused intention**. Focused intention is simply holding a thought
and the emotion associated with it
regularly and consistently enough
so that you can begin to see it manifest in your life. Our thoughts
don't really create our reality; it is
the vibration and emotions behind
them that do. Write down what you
want in as much detail as possible.
Refine your list at least quarterly.

The act of writing creates a great deal of focus that helps the manifestation process.

Here's an example. One of my patients, whom I'll call Eleanor, had been working on her marriage for years. Finally, in desperation, she decided to take her focus off trying to change her husband. Instead, she wrote down all the characteristics she was looking for in a relationship and divided them into categories such as companionship, emotions, relationships with her children, money, physical appearance, and so on. She then stated them out loud to some of her friends and to the universe in general. This began a process of putting her intentions out to the universe. Eleanor got very excited by this process. It was freeing and fun.

By describing exactly how she wanted to feel in a relationship and including details about everything she could think of, Eleanor was sending a powerful vibration out into the universe that she hoped would attract what she was looking for.

You can do the same thing with any area of your life—be it a business, a home, a car, or whatever.

2. Allow the universe to help you. Once you've stated your intention to the universe, you have to get out of the way and let universal law take over to assist you. And guess what? You won't be able to control how it will happen. Think of it this way. God has a huge staff, none of whom are waiting for their benefits. They will help you, but first you have to ask, and then you have to allow what you asked for to come.

I've come to see that our prayers are always answered. It's just that our egos often can't recognize that fact until much later, once the dust has settled. After Eleanor wrote down her relationship goals, she put them away in her journal and simply read them once a week.

3. Be prepared for growth, change, and perhaps, some pain. Caroline Myss once said, "It's a day at the beach for an angel to wipe out a marriage or a job in a single day." What she meant by that statement is that many times the first step to getting what we really want will be the painful process of losing what no longer serves us. Grief is almost inevitable when we lose something we gave significant amounts of time and energy to in the hopes that things would turn out differently. Many times, too, we long for something new and better in our lives, but cling to old patterns out of fear, greed, or an outmoded idea of how our lives are supposed to look. But when our intent to change is strong enough and we get clear, our higher selves or the angels will often orchestrate circumstances for us that force us to let go of what has become obsolete.

The first thing that happened to my patient Eleanor as a result of her clear intention is that her marriage ended. She had to go through some grieving and wailing, and work through her fears of growing old alone. But she eventually came to see that what she was really grieving was not the actual relationship she had with her husband, but instead, an idea about what the relationship could become "if he would only change and get happy." Like many of us, Eleanor had to give up a fantasy, and that was harder to let go of than her actual marriage!

4. Understand the old adage: "God moves mountains; bring a shovel." The universe is there to help us, but we have to show up and do our part. I can visualize going to Boston for days. To get there, I either have to buy a bus or plane ticket, or get in my car and drive. Eleanor had to move mountains by forcing herself to go through the paperwork and financial documentation that constitute all legal proceedings. She told me that as long as she saw it as a meditation, she didn't get overwhelmed by the process.

5. Be patient, be vulnerable, but don't be stupid. When we let go of the old and begin to imagine the possibility of something better, we are in a vulnerable in-between state. We must allow ourselves to stay right where we are and embrace our vulnerability as a chance to live fully. As Pema Chödrön writes in her wonderfully comforting book, *When Things Fall Apart* (Shambhala 1997): "Life is a good teacher and a good friend. Things are always in transition, if we could only realize it. Nothing ever sums itself up in the way that

we like to dream about. The off-center, in-between state is an ideal situation, a situation in which we don't get caught, and in which we can open our hearts and minds beyond limit."

If we learn how to move toward the pain and grief of life's inevitable loss and change, and embrace it with what Chödrön refers to as unconditional friendliness, then we have a chance to really move on and change. If we harden our hearts or collapse in fear, however, we're likely to sabotage ourselves by reverting back to the old tried-and-true, but obsolete, patterns. Eleanor could assuage her fears by trying to replace her husband with another man. And if she doesn't wait until she's healed, the new man is liable to be very much like the one she just left. But if Eleanor or you or I use her "falling apart" time wisely, she will emerge stronger and healthier than ever before. This is the challenge and gift of the new millennium.

❄ ❄ ❄

*We move into the boundless energy
of freedom and joy.*

*We learn how to apply the laws of the
universe to our daily lives.*

*The Law of Attraction brings only
good into our lives.*

*We prosper as we learn to cooperate with
the Law of Abundance.*

*We are willing to let go of what has
become obsolete in our lives.*

*We allow Life to become a meditation,
and we are at peace.*

*We are preparing to enjoy
the new millennium.*

❈   ❈   ❈

"I first heard of John Randolph Price
when he created the World Healing
Meditation in December 1986. On
December 31st of that year, more than
500 million people came together in
consciousness to meditate on peace and
love. I had the privilege of meeting this
kind, funloving man and his dear wife,
Jan, and I stayed at their Texas home.
It was love at first sight. They have both
been spreading a powerful message of love
and healing for many years. His ability to
touch the hearts of millions and help them
connect with their own greatness has been
a positive contribution to the world.
He is an inspiration to all of us."

— Louise L. Hay

❈   ❈   ❈

My Vision of the Year 2000

❧ John Randolph Price ❧

A s we cross the bridge to the year 2000, I see great change taking place as individuals and groups prepare for the new millennium. Some see only a positive future, a bright light shining on the horizon, and are filled with love and joy in anticipation of this special moment in history. Others are not quite so sure. There is a degree of apprehension, forcing them to look at priorities in life, make major decisions, face change as best they can, and try to get into the next century with as little trauma and as few scars as possible.

Then there are those with the common perception that we will soon move through the darkness of the terrible times as a prelude to either facing or escaping God's judgment. Newspaper ads tell us how to be prepared for Jesus' return and the rescue of his people. A videotape forecasts the end of the world—a repeat of the year 999, when thousands gathered in Rome to wait for the grand finale. An apocalyptic cult plans violent acts at the end of 1999 "to bring Jesus back to life." Newsletters predict the trials and tribulations to come with respect to famines and wars. And of course, the upcoming Y2K "disaster" is being talked about from pulpits to boardrooms.

Who is right? Everyone is, by "right of consciousness." Each one of us will experience what we are holding in mind and heart—what we truly believe.

I'm not saying that those beliefs will be played out exactly as they are held in consciousness, but fear will draw fearful conditions, doom-and-gloom thinking will attract that energy into personal lives, and the self-fulfilling prophecies from various religious persuasions may well stir up provocative situations for the "end times."

Even the ones who are holding their breath as we move toward January 1, 2000, in a stockpile and survivalist mentality—wishing for the best but fearing the worst—are going to find a sense of greater paranoia creeping into their daily lives. In one way or another, they will experience their prophecy of troubles.

And those who think that things will get even better in the year 2000? The same principle applies. "You are what you think about all day long," said Emerson. When we dwell on the truth that this is a loving universe where every good and perfect possibility exists, we are moving to a higher frequency in consciousness and finer experiences in life. When we focus on that which is good in this world, the positive aspects of our individual lives are multiplied. *Energy follows thought.* What we give our attention to, whether positive or negative, grows. What we see we shall become. We have a choice.

The choice that I have made for the new century is one of great joy. I see with excited delight a positive chain reaction in humanity's collective consciousness where peace comes forth in every mind, love flows forth from every heart, forgiveness reigns in every soul, and understanding is the common bond. Yes, those words are from the World Healing Meditation that began on December 31, 1986, when more than 500 million people came together in one moment in time to think peace, radiate love, and release spiritual energy for the good of all. And you know what happened.

Within months, Gorbachev urged openness and reconstruction for the Soviet Union, called for government elections, and met with President Reagan to ban nuclear weapons in Europe. A year later, the International Peace Research Institute in Stockholm reported that "1988 has seen remarkable progress toward a potentially more peaceful world." And in 1989 the Berlin Wall came down, and Eastern Europe came out of the cold and joined a new global society.

If millions more will gather on December 31, 1999, to focus their light on the countdown to 2000, the result will again be spectacular. The Y2K bug will be seen as worry-about-nothing, the doomsday prophets will go into hiding with millions deserting their apocalyptic groups, and the alarmists will find their websites in complete disfavor. In time, we will find a new sense of spiritual freedom as religions enter into a spirit of cooperation, and the idea of "unity through diversity" will be universally acknowledged. There will be a new blend of science and spirit, with great emphasis placed on nontraditional mental-emotional healing as a return to health. The global economy will flourish, international conflicts will diminish, and the political arena in America will focus on solidarity with the dawn of a new conscience—with the people responding with optimism and self-confidence.

When my wife, Jan, was beyond the veil during her near-death experience, she saw the light of Planet Earth growing and spreading, and she knew with all her heart that this world is being lifted into a higher and finer vibration. And it begins with individuals like you and me—seeing rightly, thinking positively, and feeling joyfully. As Benjamin Franklin said, "Do not anticipate trouble, or worry about what may never happen. Keep in the sunlight."

Here is an affirmative meditation that will help us stay in that sunlight as we move toward the new millennium:

I turn away from sadness and sorrow, from worry and concern, from conflict and chaos. I know this is a benevolent universe and that I was created to live in gladness, abundance, and harmony.

I make my choice now to live lovingly, joyfully, and peacefully—to smile and laugh and sing as I embrace the fullness of life—

*doing everything for the incredible
joy and fun of it.*

*I toss worry behind, wave anxiety out of
the way, and tell fear it no longer has a
place in my consciousness. I am willing to
be happy for the rest of my life.*

🌀   🌀   🌀

*We see a bright light shining
on the horizon.*

This is a loving universe, and we are loved.

*We anticipate a new century
of joy with delight.*

*Love and understanding is our
common bond.*

We focus our light on the year 2000.

*We respond to life with optimism
and confidence.*

"Carol Ritberger, Ph.D., is a joyfully alive woman. Her smile radiates love. We were only in each other's company for a few minutes when it seemed as though we had been friends for a long time. Our first luncheon was filled with laughter as we saw the humor in every situation. Her ability to see someone's aura change and to practically read their thoughts takes a bit of getting used to. But it is fun."

— **Louise L. Hay**

XIII

The Dawn of a New Light

🕯 **Carol Ritberger, Ph.D.** 🕯

We are standing at the threshold of a time of compelling change. A positive major shift is taking place, which is having a dramatic impact on our lives. We are talking about it and seeking to understand it. It is causing dynamic changes to occur within the physical body and the human energy system, and it is awakening a new energy force within each of us. We are changing to forms of light that are not as we have known them; and we are becoming more vibrant, more radiant, and more empowered. This new ener-

gy force is changing our way of thinking and is illuminating a whole new
dimension of our persona. We are
being nudged, pushed, and driven to
learn more about who we really are. It
is creating the need for intense self-
exploration and is fueling the desire to
better understand ourselves. Its energy
is assisting us in learning how to get in
touch with our deeper inner selves.

This energy force is encouraging us
to remember that we each have something unique to contribute to life, and it
is teaching us how to reconnect ourselves with that Divine essence called
Spirit. Spirit is the childlike part of us
that remembers that life is to be
enjoyed and that every challenge we
face is the opportunity to learn more
about who we are. Spirit is the perpet-
ual optimist that fills our lives with joy
and creates the healing energy of hope.
It is through our spiritual self that the

miracle of true healing is possible.

Perhaps one of the most challenging aspects of this dynamic new energy force is that it is influencing our thinking and affecting out behavior. We are being reminded that we alone are responsible for the directions of our lives and our physical well-being. We are being inspired to look beyond the obvious and that which our five senses can offer. This new energy force is sensitizing us to the need to develop our thinking in such a way that our mental processing is the same, but the way we perceive our lives is going through a radical change. Consciousness, as we have known it, is expanding. We are being guided to no longer see the world from the perspective of two- or even three-dimensional consciousness, for it limits us and inhibits our growth. These states of consciousness only allow us to see ourselves as progressing or regressing, or to see things only as black or white, right or wrong. The result is an increased sense of alienation and a feeling of disconnection from our higher self.

The energetic force of the millennium is causing a third and new way of thinking to emerge. That way of thinking is called telekinetic consciousness, which is the bridge that allows us to access fourth-dimensional reality. In this state of reality, there is no duality, just oneness. There is neither beginning nor end. The mind is no longer restricted to a conscious or subconscious way of perceiving, but is simultaneous and whole in its functioning. The use of intuition is no longer an occasional occurrence, but becomes an integral aspect of our decision-making patterns. In this realm of consciousness, the rules are different. The boundaries of thinking are no longer linear, but are geometric and are formed only by the choices we make. Space and time, as we have known them, cease to create balance—balance that is necessary to heal ourselves and sustain good health in the new world that lies before us.

When we direct our energies into the realm of fourth-dimensional reality, we enter into what the Ancients called "high alchemy." We activate our ethereal chakras and initiate a new source of light and energy. This alchemical transformation accelerates the expansion and integration of intuition and creates a sense of spiritual purification and clarification. Our identity is no longer a matter of what we do to earn a living, but energetic patterns of light that reflect our higher Divine self, our authenticity, and our intentions. The old patterns of thought that have limited and inhibited us no longer exist. Our awareness becomes heightened, so we can recognize the patterns of behavior that prevent us from attaining the abundance we desire and deserve. We begin to reconstruct our personal ways of thinking that are responsible for the creation of imbalance and illness. We become conscious observers of the choices we make and how those choices affect the direction of our lives. We integrate the healing energy of hope into our lives, and we illuminate the wholeness of our being.

The energy force of the millennium offers us the opportunity to make tremendous breakthroughs in learning how to utilize our different degrees of consciousness. It offers positive change to all who are open and receptive. It holds within it the keys that can unlock the mysteries of the mind and reveal the steps we must take in order to tap into the vast realm of spiritual wisdom—wisdom without boundaries.

The choice is ours. The rewards are many. The beneficiaries are the members of the human race.

We are becoming more vibrant, more radiant, and more empowered.

Intuition is now an everyday aspect of our decision-making process.

This is a time for tremendous breakthroughs in consciousness.

We are now able to tap into the vast realm of spiritual wisdom.

⊛   ⊛   ⊛

"Ron Roth enjoys good food almost as much as I do. We have had many a good meal together. I met Ron several years ago when he timidly came to the Hayride, my AIDS support group. He was so nervous to be in the room with people with AIDS. I was excited to have a priest (which he was at the time) visit us, so I made him get up and say something inspirational to these frightened young men. At the end of the meeting, lots of the boys came up to Ron to thank him for being there. We lose our fears by jumping into the fire."

— Louise L. Hay

⊛   ⊛   ⊛

Millennium 2000: A Time for Hope

Ron Roth, Ph.D.

One evening recently, after a somewhat taxing day, I sat down, picked up the TV remote, and clicked on the set, hoping to find some relaxing entertainment.

The channel I happened to tune in to featured a program that immediately began to assault my senses with sound bites from doomsday cult members spouting their frightful millennium predictions about the Y2K virus and how it was the beginning of the end. Incidentally, I didn't stay tuned in long enough to find out what it was that was possibly coming to an end. Hopefully, it is the end to all of these prophecies of gloom and doom that are getting so much media attention today.

Unfortunately, most of these fear-based "prophecies" are coming from people who ought to know better—individuals who are claiming to be "inspired by God." As one who once worked in the area of institutional religion, I would disagree with these purveyors of guilt and shame in their understanding of the ancient meaning of the word *prophet*. In religious history, a prophet was one who "spoke forth" good news concerning God's love. Sometimes this good news included "visions" of possible cataclysmic events if people continued to exist in the negative energies of fear, hate, anger, bitterness, and resentment—thought patterns not conducive to receiving the "love energy" of the Divine that "resides" at the center of our being.

How does one transform one's negative, fearful energy into positive, loving energy?

From a practical viewpoint, don't allow yourself to buy into any of this fear-based thinking. This type of negative thinking will simply breed more fear. Think and affirm the fact that *love* is the energy that creates healing. This way of thinking will breed *more* love, as well as peace and harmony. In your prayers and meditations, you can release this healing energy to the entire planet by affirming, "I bless the earth and all the creatures with loving kindness." In fact, you can repeat this affirmation often throughout the day.

And finally, follow up the above meditation with the practice of loving kindness. Ask yourself during your morning prayer, "How may I help? How may I be an instrument of peace?" Intuitively, you will be guided by the still, small voice that is Divine within you. This is the voice that will help you remember, "Fear not, I AM with you."

In my studies of the Sacred Scriptures, I once discovered that there were 365 admonitions in these sacred writings of the Hebrew and Christian testaments encouraging people not to be afraid—one admonition for each day of the year!

As we approach the next millennium, I believe that it's time to heed these positive words of hope, knowing that the greatest contribution we can make to life is not our thoughts and words filled with fear, but our thoughts and actions imbued with *love*.

In the final analysis, what is important to experiencing life to the fullest is not just what we were and what we did for one another, but how much love we put into the doing.

*Love is the most powerful
healing force there is.*

Together we create millennium love.

We tap into the love energy of the Divine.

*Love brings peace and harmony
to this millennium.*

*I am an instrument of peace for
the new century.*

*Our thoughts and actions are filled
with love for all of life.*

❧   ❧   ❧

"I often remember the wonderful afternoon I spent with Mona Lisa Schulz at the Aquarium in Chicago. We found the penguin exhibit and sat enthralled for quite some time watching the penguin families going about their business. It was a very special time for both of us. Like me, Mona Lisa also loves to feed the birds. We both have several bird feeders around our homes and are fascinated by their joy in finding extra food."

— Louise L. Hay

❧   ❧   ❧

Medicine for the Next Millennium

🐢 Mona Lisa Schulz, M.D., Ph.D. 🐢

Some people are really scared about the coming millennium. Fear-filled stories of apocalyptic change and destruction are common. From my perspective, each of us needs to know that true intuition is different from fear. And when we learn how to tell the difference between the two, we need not get derailed by excessive fear. Fear is an emotion that signals that you are entering into an unfamiliar or unknown place where something new is about to happen. Our fears have a way of mushrooming and spiraling into something bigger than they have to be depending on how we and our bodies interpret them. We might, for example, believe that the new and unfamiliar will cause us to lose control, become helpless, be hurt or harmed in some way, experience danger, or lose something valuable. When we allow our intuition to be clouded by fear, we run the risk of creating a world that is filled with inescapable danger.

Misinterpreting the coming changes of the new millennium through a veil of fear is what gets so many people all riled up. Every one of us is likely in the coming year or two to experience some type of fear, large or small, which is being triggered by the momentum and energy of the next millennium. I like to call these feelings mini-millennium experiences. When you know what these experiences are and why you're having them, your fear will gradually evaporate, and you'll come to see how rich and full your life can truly be.

As we enter the new millennium, all of us can expect experiences that mirror the wisdom of the Tarot: All areas of bondage that no longer serve us must go through the shattering changes of the Tower so that we can experience the grace of the Start. And that is what the new millennium brings to us: the opportunity to discard the old ways of being that may well have served us in the past, but will no longer help us in the future. We will all be asked to leave behind old relationships and old patterns of behavior so that we can bring newness into our lives. This almost always involves fear, feeling some pain, and then, ultimately, enjoying the sense

of calm, peace, and new beginnings
that mark the promise of the next millennium.

❧   ❧   ❧

*We allow fear to evaporate and
know that we are safe.*

*We discard old ways of being that
no longer serve us.*

We bring wonderful newness into our lives.

*We eagerly await the new beginnings that
mark this new millennium.*

✤ ✤ ✤

"I have known and respected
Dr. Bernie Siegel from the moment
I first met him. I still have my first
copy of <u>Love, Medicine & Miracles</u> from
1986. It is thoroughly dog-eared, with
many passages highlighted with my
yellow marker. I used to carry it everywhere. When I spoke in public, I would
read to my audiences from the book. In
those days, I was just a crazy lady with
crazy ideas. I was so excited to find a
medical doctor validating what I had
been saying for some time. Bernie is a
very wise and wonderful man."

— **Louise L. Hay**

✤ ✤ ✤

XVI

A Millennium Message

🕷 Bernie S. Siegel, M.D. 🕷

*What is a man that thou are mindful
of him? And the son of man, that
thou visitest him? For thou hast made
him a little lower than the angels, and
hast crowned him with glory and
honor. Thou madest him to have
dominion over the works of thy hands;
thou hast put all things under his feet.*

— Psalm 8

🕷　🕷　🕷

My hope is that in the next millennium, the human race will finally step up and accept its responsibilities. We will no longer see our differences as something to fight and kill over, but we'll see our similarities. It is time to accept the fact that we are all the same color inside and have the same parents, Adam and Eve. Religions, in the next millennium, will hopefully become pathways to God—as they were meant to be—and not sources of war.

When we accept that we are co-creators here to extend God's love, compassion, and empathy to all living things, we will create a Garden of Eden on Earth. A Garden of Eden without free will is meaningless, but when free will is present and life's difficulties exist, the extension of love from one living thing to another becomes the greatest healing force that all existing life can experience.

Read Corinthians 1:13 and become aware of the power and the qualities of love: *"And now abideth faith, hope, love, these three; but the greatest of these is love."*

To survive, we need faith in the true Lord, Who created us out of love to extend that love to all of creation. We also need hope if we are to go on, but the hope and the faith are sustained by the love we must begin to show for each other and all forms of life.

From nothing, the great undifferentiated potential, came the One, who created us all. It is not a mystery to me that the number 10 is so symbolic. The One and the Zero. The entire computer system relies on it. Our Ten Commandments, a minyan, fingers and toes, perfect test scores, and so on. The

10 is the sum of all our relationships and meanings. 1+2+3+4 = 10. When we all come together, we will find wholeness in the next millennium.

I pray that it be so. The solution to our problems lies not in outer space, but inside us all. Our past is in space, but our future is within us. When the gods hid wisdom, they put it where they knew the human race would rarely look. No, it is not on mountaintops, beneath the sea, or under the earth. They hid it inside of all of us. Let us stop being afraid to go within. Let us stop projecting evil to others. Let us accept our shadows and imperfections, and eliminate them with the light of love.

Jonah cried from the belly of a whale. God heard and answered. We will be heard, too, if we raise our voices in the name of faith, hope, and love. God has asked me to leave you with this parable: We are satellite dishes, remote controls, and television screens. Please take that to heart. If you have trouble, as I do, with parables, let me help you. We are receivers of the Word, but what word or channel do you tune in to? You have a heart and mind that you can use to select the channel that you should listen to. Let it be The Voice of God, and then use your body like a television screen to manifest your beliefs with the proper action. Deeds are the key, not idle words. Live your love, and the world will be healed. Actions speak louder than words.

Understand, forgive, and love yourself. Love your families, love your neighbors, love your friends and strangers, and love your enemies. They deserve it now. It will heal you, them, and our planet.

We see our similarities in everyone
and rejoice in them.

As co-creators, we envision a true
Garden of Eden here on Earth.

The power of love permeates every person,
place, and thing on this planet.

Our future resides in our
hearts and minds.

We tune into the positive
channels of wisdom.

We live our love, and the world is healed.

❧   ❧   ❧

"As a fellow dedicated, organic gardener, Donald Trotter won my heart the first time I met him. We were soon talking gardens and sharing ideas. Donald was impressed that I was such a good gardener, and I was impressed by the vast amount of knowledge he had. I always look forward to his frequent e-mails with bits of new gardening knowledge and a joke or two. We both believe in healing the planet by nurturing the precious bits of earth we have the privilege of cultivating."

— **Louise L. Hay**

❧   ❧   ❧

XVII

Earthkeeping: A Word for the New Millennium

🖦 Donald W. Trotter, Ph.D. 🖦

Hello, fellow Earthlings, and welcome to the new millennium party. As we all embark on this journey into the 21st century, I'd like to speak to you about a word I thought up recently: *Earthkeeping*. It may take the rest of my life to fully grasp the meaning of this newly formed noun, but it certainly is a word for the new millennium.

We human beings have our work cut out for us in so many ways as we form the clay that will be our legacy for the generations to follow. While this evolution takes place, we must not forget that no matter how advanced our technologies become, nature and the natural world will never be obsolete. This planet has been our home, and we will be asked to be better Earthkeepers if we intend it to be our home in the future. As our technologies grow in spirit, the one constant will be Earth. While we are making affirmations about love, personal growth, love, spiritual awareness, love, responsibilities, love, shouldn't the environment that sustains us also be included in this mantra?

Take a moment and think about some of the most incredible and breathtaking things that you have witnessed in your life. Is nature or some natural wonder in there somewhere?

We are fed, clothed, and sheltered

by this amazing orb spinning through space. Earth is such a precious and unique phenomenon, and we are so very fortunate to inhabit such a place. I wonder if we sometimes forget how rare and extraordinary we humans are. We are capable of such deep feelings and so much loveliness. This is all made possible by our Earth and the nature we call Mother. As we hurry along in order to pay our bills, raise our children, and grow into better people, Earth waits patiently for us to partake in her beauty and her bounty.

In the coming century, let us endeavor to understand and appreciate our planet so that we may better comprehend the new worlds we are destined to encounter as we look to the stars. To gain this knowledge of our planet, we must develop respect for the fantastic diversity of living organisms that inhabit her, along with us. With this respect, together we can heal what we have damaged, and nurture Mother Earth, who has nurtured *us* for so long.

Earthkeeping—a word for the next millennium.

We are all becoming better Earthkeepers.

We are grateful for the beauty the
earth constantly gives us.

We appreciate our planet in
new ways every day.

We take loving care of our
precious environment.

We nurture Mother Earth,
who nurtures us all.

❧ ❧ ❧

"If you want to have a real fun time,
hang out with Stuart Wilde. He has the
most unexpected sense of humor. I am
always laughing when I am with him.
I have never known anyone who can get
into more silly situations or find more
unusual solutions to getting out of them.
Stuart sees life through eyes
that see how foolish we all are."

— Louise L. Hay

❧ ❧ ❧

XVIII

Faith in a Balanced Planet

❂ Stuart Wilde ❂

The actual start of the new millennium is an arbitrary date. Most historians say that Jesus was born in 4 B.C., and 11 days were knocked off the Gregorian calendar in the Middle Ages. So, in fact, the new millennium began in late 1996.

However, the advent of the millennium is still impacting us, as it allows many to acknowledge their fears and express their darker side. That is why apocalyptic merchandising is running hot and heavy; many organizations are *selling* the end of the world. You can even buy maps channeled by psychics that indicate which bits of America and the rest of the world will be underwater once the earth changes happen.

Water is an archetypal symbol of emotion. When people feel restricted and overwhelmed by change and the pace of life, they imagine cataclysm and floods. I don't believe the world is going to end. In fact, I see the millennium as a positive thing. It allows us to look at who we are and where we're going.

In the next generation, you will see a push-pull process between those who seek to perpetuate consumerism and industrial growth, and those of opposite persuasions who will warn of the need to simplify, conserve, and restrain the forward march of materialism and economic growth.

It will be interesting to see how it works out. It's yang versus yin. The ecosystem of our planet badly needs the yin team to win, for the levels of toxicity from PCBs, dioxins, and other estrogen-mimicking chemicals in the food chain seem to be causing irreparable damage to animal and human reproduction.

In America, the birth rate has fallen to a break-even point. In Europe, it is well below replacement levels, except in Ireland and Spain. In Asia, it's still well ahead of replacement levels; however, fertility is dropping dramatically all over the world.

Perhaps this is how the planet looks after itself. Once enough pollutants enter the body fat of humans, the reproduction rate drops, and industrial activity slows down everything, returning the planet to balance.

I'm batting on the yin team. I don't trust our drinking water, so I've installed filtering and reverse osmosis systems at home. I try to eat only organic foods, as I don't trust the process of mass market food production. I believe that simplicity and the sensible approach will eventually win, but the yang team will be well ahead until halftime. The ecological impact of consumerism will become ever more marked, and we will either voluntarily change or it will be forced upon us.

Either way, I'm pretty sure the planet will be okay in the end. The earth is a self-organizing system—it has a spirit, much the same as we have spirits, evolving inside our human form. The earth spirit knows how to balance itself, after all, and it has kept itself growing and evolving for more than four billion years through conditions that were often much worse than the current situation.

Spirituality, minimalism, softness, and the yin way of life represent an expression whose time has not yet come—but it will.

The earth is a self-organizing system.

This planet knows how to balance and heal itself.

Earth has been here for billions of years and will continue.

We are safe, and all is well in our world.

❀ ❀ ❀

"In the early days of the AIDS epidemic, Marianne Williamson and I were both at the forefront of trying to help people cope with this dis-ease. We both held weekly meetings in the Los Angeles area. Since the meetings were held on different nights, many of the same people were able to attend both. Marianne began Project Angel Food to provide meals for those who were suffering from the illness and had no money for food. Those days have given us memories that we will carry for the rest of our lives."

— **Louise L. Hay**

❀ ❀ ❀

Choices in the Third Millennium

🕸 Marianne Williamson 🕸

As we count the days until the third millennium, it feels more and more as though we're approaching a fork in the road of human history. On one side, I see enchantment, illumination, and spiritual bliss. On the other, I see dark clouds looming over the human race, and destruction and devastation on unimaginable levels. As awed as I am by the prospect of either vision coming to pass, I feel one thing deeply: "These are your choices. Each one of you must choose."

Who among us doesn't wish to see humanity take the higher road, the peaceful path to an Earth becoming one with heaven. Yet at this point, if that's going to happen, it will only be because we make it so. The true choice for love takes, on some level, personal courage; forgiveness is a radical departure from the status quo mentality of our time. Imagine a declaration by the U.S. government that the purpose of the United States is that we might experience love for each other and all the world. Imagine the health and happiness of the children of the world becoming our ultimate objective. Imagine the eradication of human suffering becoming our highest goal. Imagine our desire and willingness to forgive each other becoming stronger than our temptation to judge and attack!

Let us imagine a better world, and turn our hearts and spiritual imaginations into a broad-scale social force for good. That, to me, is the meaning of the millennium: We can have whatever we want to have, and we *will* have whatever we choose. Let's choose hope. Let's choose peace. Let's choose forgiveness. Let's choose love.

Humanity now takes the high road.

Our purpose is to experience love for each other and for the whole world.

We now eradicate all human suffering.

We move into a millennium of love.

Final Thoughts

In the coming millennium, I see positive changes occurring in every phase of life, particularly the health field. For example, retirement homes will include holistic health centers. In addition to traditional doctors and nurses, there will be a prevalence of chiropractors, acupuncturists, homeopaths, traditional Chinese medicine practitioners, nutritionists, herbologists, massage therapists, and yoga teachers. It will be a time when everyone can look forward to healthy, carefree years as they grow older.

I know from the vast correspondence I receive from people all over the world that many people are ready for positive changes and are willing to learn a new way of thinking and believing. As Ken Carey says in his book *The New Millennium,* "The warm rains of New Thought fall gently on the soil of human consciousness."

The old prophecies that predicted gloom and doom for humanity were written when human consciousness was much different. In the last 20 years, humanity has had an enormous shifting of beliefs, and the old prophecies no longer hold true. I say to those who point to ancient texts to predict our future, "Just because something is ingrained in you does not make it true." Remember, we once believed that the world was flat. We can heal and go beyond our limiting societal beliefs that predict a millennium rife with fear and danger. To me, the millennium is just a number and really has no meaning at all. Much depends on what calendar you're using. The calendar we're now using in America is actually a corrected version of the Gregorian calendar.

So, you can see that we now have a choice of which path to take. We can think fearful thoughts, or we can align our thinking with the glorious possibilities Life has in store for us. The future is up to us. We have the power to bring peace to everyone on the planet. We have the power to heal nature and quiet the tremblings of the earth. We have the power to heal our children and make Life safe for all of them. We have the power to make war an outdated thing of the past. We have the power to feed, clothe, house, and educate everyone, everywhere.

This coming millennium will be a reflection of what is in our hearts and minds. Come join me and millions of others in creating the mental atmosphere on this planet that will   bring only good and expansive experiences for us all.

We can now move forward in life to our greatest opportunities and challenges—knowing that *all is well!*

※   ※   ※

Affirmations for the Year 2000 and Beyond

We radiate success, and we prosper wherever we turn.

The year 2000 is a time of wonderful new beginnings.

We live from the belief that we are here to "bless and prosper each other."

The safety we seek in the outer world begins with the safety we create within ourselves.

We apply fresh new thinking in this new century and have fresh new experiences.

*We have chosen to incarnate at this
particular time to be part of the
healing process of the planet.*

*This is the beginning of the best
century of all time.*

*The new millennium brings us only
good, positive experiences.*

*The year 2000 opens a new era of
freedom and positive growth.*

*We are given new information to
live in new positive ways.*

*We are always safe and Divinely
protected and guided.*

*Our understanding of Life and how
to live it deepens and grows.*

*We learn to love and support each other,
and our way is made easy.*

*We love waking up to greet each bright new
day in the new millennium.*

*This new century is like no century we have
ever known before.*

*We only think thoughts about what we
really do want in our lives.*

*We choose to think thoughts that
make us feel good.*

*Our good is constantly coming to us so we
can relax and enjoy our new life.*

*We are free of the restrictions of the past
and are ready to enjoy the new era.*

197

*Any challenges we have are merely
passing events, and all really is
well in our world.*

*We are constantly redefining who we are
and how we want to live.*

*What we choose to think and do today has
an effect on our future.*

We are powerful creators in our world.

*We accept opportunities as they
come our way.*

We feel confident about our future.

*We take the time to help make the
planet a better place to live.*

*Our loving thoughts connect with those
of like-minded people, and together
we help to heal the planet.*

198 🏵

*Whenever we hear of a disaster, we
always send loving, healing thoughts
to those involved.*

*As we release the past, we embrace
ourselves and life in a whole new light of
freedom, compassion, joy, and love.*

*We surrender to the positive new
changes in our lives. We are safe and
supported at all times.*

*Our children are always surrounded by
healthy, happy, supportive people.*

*We trust our inner guidance.
It shows us the best way to live.*

*We now move into a new era of prosperity
and abundance. Thank you, Life.*

The wisdom of the Universe resides in each of my children, and they are safe.

We are developing a strong faith in ourselves and in life.

In this new century, only good will come.

We move beyond the past and now experience a bright, loving, prosperous new future.

The past is over and done, and only good lies before us.

We trust the process of Life.

Every choice we make from now on is the perfect choice for us.

Our compassion for all of Life helps to heal the planet.

*We are in the right place at the right time
doing the right thing.*

*We are under the law of our own conscious-
ness, for our thoughts create our lives.*

*Our harmonious thoughts create a
harmonious, loving Life.*

*We willingly release any need for struggle
or suffering. We deserve all that is good.*

*All of our friends and family members are
Divinely protected at all times.*

*We envision a world of love and kindness,
and we do our best to contribute to
this loving world.*

*Today we deepen our understanding so
that we may comprehend more of Life.*

The world is being made a safe place
for all women and children, and we
contribute to that safety.

We are at peace with the positive changes
that the new millennium brings into our lives.

We now create a loving world in our minds.
That which is within us must unfold
in our outer world.

We are constantly aware of our close
connection with the Universe and
with all of Life.

We now flow with the perfect
unfoldment of our lives.

With joy and anticipation, we welcome
new experiences into our lives.

*We are open, relaxed, and free.
We dwell in the present time with ease.*

*That which is for our highest good
now unfolds perfectly before us.*

*Everything in our experience continually
improves. We are balanced, peaceful,
and happy.*

*It is such fun creating wonderful new
lives for ourselves. We enjoy thinking
new thoughts.*

*We recognize our true worth and know that
all is abundantly well in our lives.*

*We are connected with Divine wisdom.
All the answers to all the questions we
shall ever ask are already within us. We
trust our own intuition.*

*Releasing all fearful thoughts, we
know that all is well in our world—
now and forevermore!*

About the Contributors

Joan Borysenko, Ph.D., has been described as a respected scientist, gifted therapist, and unabashed mystic. Trained at Harvard Medical School, where she was an instructor in medicine until 1988, she is a pioneer in mind/body medicine, women's health, and the author of several books, including the bestsellers *Minding the Body, Mending the Mind; The Power of the Mind to Heal; A Woman's Book of Life;* and *The Ways of the Mystic.*

❧ ❧ ❧

Carolyn A. Bratton is the co-founder of the Lifestream Center, Roanoke, Virginia's only holistic healing center; and she is an ordained minister as well. A graduate of two of Louise Hay's

Intensive Training Programs, for several years Carolyn has been conducting workshops and seminars in both the United States and abroad based on Louise's bestseller *You Can Heal Your Life* and James Redfield's book *The Celestine Prophecy*.

❊   ❊   ❊

Sylvia Browne's incredible psychic powers have been witnessed by millions of people on TV shows such as *Montel Williams* and *Unsolved Mysteries*. She has been profiled on numerous national news programs; and her on-target psychic readings astound audiences wherever she appears. Sylvia is the president of the Sylvia Browne Corporation, and the founder of the church, Society of Novus Spiritus, located in Campbell, California. She is the *New York Times* bestselling author of *Adventures of a Psychic.*

❧   ❧   ❧

Deepak Chopra, **M.D.**, is Chief Executive Officer of The Chopra Center for Well Being in La Jolla, California. He is a bestselling author whose many works include *The Seven Spiritual Laws of Success; Quantum Healing; Ageless Body, Timeless Mind;* and *The Path to Love.* Formerly Chief of Staff at New England Memorial Hospital, he also taught at Tufts University and Boston University Schools of Medicine. Recognized for his role in bringing time-honored Eastern principles to the Western world, he is an internationally acclaimed speaker; and his television programs appear frequently on PBS stations. Dr. Chopra currently teaches mind/body techniques and educational programs worldwide.

❧   ❧   ❧

Alan Cohen is the author of 14 popular inspirational books, including the classic *The Dragon Doesn't Live Here Anymore* and the award-winning *A Deep Breath of Life*; he is a contributing writer for the *New York Times* bestselling series *Chicken Soup for the Soul.* Alan resides in Maui, Hawaii, where he conducts seminars on spiritual awakening and visionary living. He also keynotes and presents seminars at conferences throughout the United States and abroad.

❧   ❧   ❧

Terah Kathryn Collins is an internationally recognized Feng Shui consultant, speaker, teacher, and bestselling author. With a background in communications and holistic health, she is the originator of Essential Feng Shui™; and founder of the Western School of Feng Shui, located in the San Diego area. Her first book, *The Western Guide to Feng Shui: Creating Balance, Harmony and Prosperity in Your Environment,* is one of the bestselling Feng Shui books in the world. She has been a featured speaker on many radio and television shows, as well as at special events including the International Feng Shui Conference and the Empowering Women seminars held in many cities across the United States.

✦   ✦   ✦

Dr. Tom Costa is founder of the Religious Science Church of the Desert in Palm Desert, California, and is currently on the Board of Directors of Religious Science International. His popularity as a public speaker has resulted in a number of television appearances, as well as lectures and seminars throughout the United States and Canada. Tom is the author of *Life! You Wanna Make Something of It?*

❧   ❧   ❧

Shakti Gawain is the bestselling author of *Creative Visualization, Living in the Light, Return to the Garden,* and a number of other bestselling books. For more than 20 years, Shakti has facilitated thousands of people in learning to trust and act on their own inner truth, thus releasing and developing their creativity in every area of their lives. Shakti and her husband, Jim Burns, are co-founders of Nataraj Publishing. They make their home in Mill Valley and on the Hawaiian island of Kauai.

❖ ❖ ❖

Louise L. Hay is a metaphysical lecturer and teacher and the bestselling author of 23 books, including *You Can Heal Your Life* and *Empowering Women*. Her works have been translated into 25 different languages in 33 countries throughout the world. Since beginning her career as a Science of Mind minister in 1981, Louise has assisted thousands of people in discovering and using the full potential of their own creative powers for personal growth and self-healing. Louise is the owner and founder of Hay House, Inc., a self-help publishing company that disseminates books, audios, and videos that contribute to the healing of the planet.

❧ ❧ ❧

Carolle Jean-Murat, M.D., is a board-certified obstetrician/gynecologist who has had a private practice in San Diego, California, since 1982. She is an assistant clinical professor at UCSD School of Medicine, and a clinical mentor for under-served students at San Diego State University. Dr. Jean-Murat is a motivational speaker who brings her message of self-empowerment to women through the print and broadcast media; and she is the author of the award-winning book *Staying Healthy: 10 Easy Steps for Women* (published in both English and Spanish); and *Menopause Made Easy: Making the Right Decisions for You*.

❧ ❧ ❧

William R. Levacy holds a B.A. in literature and has been a practitioner of Vedic astrology or *Jyotish,* as it is called in India, for more than 15 years. Bill received a master's degree in the Science of Creative Intelligence in 1977 from Maharishi European Research University, where he concentrated his studies on Vedic science. His 15 years of experience as a business consultant in the aerospace industry contributes to the practical, yet personal nature of his astrological readings; and is reflected in his practical work on Vedic astrology, *Beneath a Vedic Sky.* Bill resides in Southern California.

    ▒   ▒   ▒

Christiane Northrup, M.D., a pioneer in her field, is an OB/GYN who helps empower women to tune into their inner wisdom and take charge of their health. She is an Assistant Clinical Professor of OB/GYN at the University of Vermont College of Medicine; the author of the bestselling book *Women's Bodies, Women's Wisdom;* and the host of two successful public television specials. Dr. Northrup lives in Yarmouth, Maine, with her husband and two teenage daughters.

❧ ❧ ❧

John Randolph Price is an internationally known award-winning author and lecturer. Formerly a CEO in the corporate world, he has devoted over a quarter of a century to researching the mysteries of ancient wisdom and incorporating those findings in the writing of many books, which include *The Abundance Book, The Superbeings,* and

With Wings As Eagles. In 1981, he and his wife, Jan, formed The Quartus Foundation, a spiritual research and communications organization now headquartered in the Texas hill country town of Boerne, near San Antonio.

❊   ❊   ❊

Carol Ritberger, Ph.D., the author of *Your Personality, Your Health,* is a medical intuitive and an innovative leader in the fields of personality typology and behavioral medicine. She has devoted 18 years to researching and teaching the understanding of personality-type behavior and how it affects people's lives and health. Her education includes personality behavioral psychology and body/mind sciences. An international speaker with a doctorate in theology, Carol offers private sessions and workshops that focus on understanding how personality, stress, and emotions contribute to the formation of illness in the body.

❄ ❄ ❄

Ron Roth, Ph.D., is an internationally known teacher, spiritual healer, and modern-day mystic. As a leading-edge voice bringing us into the new millennium, he has appeared on many television and radio programs, including *The Oprah Winfrey Show*. Ron is the author of several books, including the bestseller *The Healing Path of Prayer* and the audiocassette *Healing Prayers*. He served in the Roman Catholic priesthood for more than 25 years and is the founder of the Celebrating Life Institute in Peru, Illinois, where he lives.

❈   ❈   ❈

Mona Lisa Schulz, M.D., Ph.D., is a neuropsychiatrist, physician-medical intuitive, and the author of *Awakening Intuition,* a practical guide for those seeking to address and heal the root patterns associated with health problems. Dr. Schulz is also an Assistant Clinical Professor of Psychiatry at the University of Vermont School of Medicine. As a medical intuitive, Dr. Schulz educates people on how emotional patterns in one's life are associated with specific illnesses in one's body. She lives in Yarmouth, Maine, with her cats Emily, Dina, and Molly.

❈   ❈   ❈

Bernie Siegel, M.D., is a retired general/pediatric surgeon who is now involved in humanizing medical care and medical education. He is the author of *Love, Medicine & Miracles; Peace, Love & Healing; How to Live Between Office Visits;* and *Prescriptions for Living*. Bernie resides in Connecticut with his wife, Bobbie.

🌀   🌀   🌀

Donald W. Trotter, Ph.D., the author of *Natural Gardening A–Z,* is a consulting horticulturist and environmental scientist. Don grew up in a family where commercial farming was a part of daily life. He pursued the love of plants shown to him by his family, and went ahead with his education in finding out how to preserve the fragile balance of nature in farming as well as in the residential garden. From the farm to the front yard, it is Don's belief that no one needs to use harmful chemicals in order to successfully tend to one's garden.

❧ ❧ ❧

Author and lecturer **Stuart Wilde** is one of the real characters of the self-help, human-potential movement. His style is humorous, controversial, poignant, and transformational. He has written 13 books, including those that make up the very successful Taos Quintet, which are considered classics in their genre. They are: *Affirmations, The Force, Miracles, The Quickening,* and *The Trick to Money Is Having Some.* Stuart's books have been translated into 12 languages.

❧ ❧ ❧

Marianne Williamson is an internationally acclaimed lecturer and the bestselling author of *A Return to Love, The Healing of America, A Woman's Worth,* and *Illuminata,* among other works. Williamson has done extensive charitable organizing throughout the country in service to people with life-challenging illnesses; and is the founder of The American Renaissance Alliance, a nonprofit grass-roots organization dedicated to introducing spiritual principles into our political discourse. She is currently the Spiritual Leader of The Church of Today, the Unity Church in Warren, Michigan.

We hope you enjoyed this Hay House book. If you would like to receive a free catalog featuring additional Hay House books and products, or if you would like information about the Hay Foundation, please contact:

Hay House, Inc.
P.O. Box 5100
Carlsbad, CA 92018-5100

(760) 431-7695 or (800) 654-5126
(760) 431-6948 (fax) or
(800) 650-5115 (fax)

Please visit the Hay House Website at:
www.hayhouse.com